Usborne
Junior
Illustrated
Grammar
and
Punctuation

Jane Bingham

Illustrated by
Alex Latimer

I'm fast.

I'm faster.

I'm the fastest!

Consultant: John Seely

Edited by Sam Taplin

Designed by Kirsty Tizzard

Quicklinks

The Usborne Quicklinks website contains
links to lots of great sites to help you with English
grammar, punctuation and spelling.

There are quizzes, word searches, puzzles
and games to practise what you know.

To visit these websites, go to

www.usborne.com/quicklinks

and type the keywords 'grammar
and punctuation'.

When using the internet, please follow
the internet safety guidelines displayed
on the Usborne Quicklinks website.

Contents

Why do we need grammar and punctuation?

Can you imagine speaking in a random jumble of words, or writing without any punctuation marks at all? Grammar and punctuation help us communicate. Without these essential tools, our words just wouldn't make sense.

What is grammar?

Grammar is a set of rules for organizing words into sentences. Each word has its own job to do, and there are clear guidelines for how words work together.

If you don't follow the rules, your writing may be hard to understand. Take a look at these two sentences:

We saw a huge plastic shark on the way to the beach.

Can you see why this sentence could be confusing?

Beach

On the way to the beach, we saw a huge plastic shark.

By rearranging the words, you can make the meaning much clearer.

What is punctuation?

Punctuation is a set of signs that are used to make writing clear. Punctuation marks divide words into groups and act as signposts, making writing easier to follow.

Sentences with no punctuation can be very confusing. For example, if you saw the sign, 'SLOW DUCKS CROSSING', you might wonder why the ducks were so slow!

If you have any doubts about why punctuation matters, try comparing the sentences below:

The children ate spaghetti ice cream and strawberries.

This sentence is missing an important comma.

The children ate spaghetti, ice cream and strawberries.

This comma changes the meaning completely.

How this book works

This book provides an easy-to-follow guide to grammar and punctuation. You can work your way through each section in order, or you can turn to the contents page and find a topic to investigate.

Rules are explained in simple language.

Example sentences are clearly labelled.

Word lists are set out in tables.

Cross-references show you where to find out more about a topic.

Panels like this contain advice on tricky words.

Test your knowledge

There are lots of quizzes throughout the book to help you practise what you've learned. Use a pen and paper for your answers. Then turn to pages 130 to 133 to see how well you've done.

Improve your writing

Would you like to make your writing more exciting? The section on writing with style (pages 102 to 113) is full of suggestions for making writing come to life. There's also a short spelling guide, starting on page 116.

Word classes

Whenever you write or talk, you put together different kinds of words. There are eight word classes and each one has its own particular job to do.

Nouns

... tell you the name of a person, an animal, a thing or a feeling.

Charlie   elephant
chocolate   happiness

Pronouns

... replace nouns, or refer to something you've already mentioned.

I   it
she   them

Adjectives

... are describing words. They give more information about something.

hairy   unusual
large   exciting

Verbs

... are 'doing' or 'being' words. Every sentence has at least one.

run   be
have   imagine

Adverbs

... tell you more about the way something is done.

rapidly   sideways
soon   carefully

Prepositions

... show the position of something or when something happened.

under   during
through   before

Conjunctions

... provide a link between different words or parts of a sentence.

and   but
because   therefore

Determiners

... come before a noun to make it clearer what you're talking about.

a   some
the   every

Using word classes

You don't often find all the word classes together, but this sentence contains all eight of them.

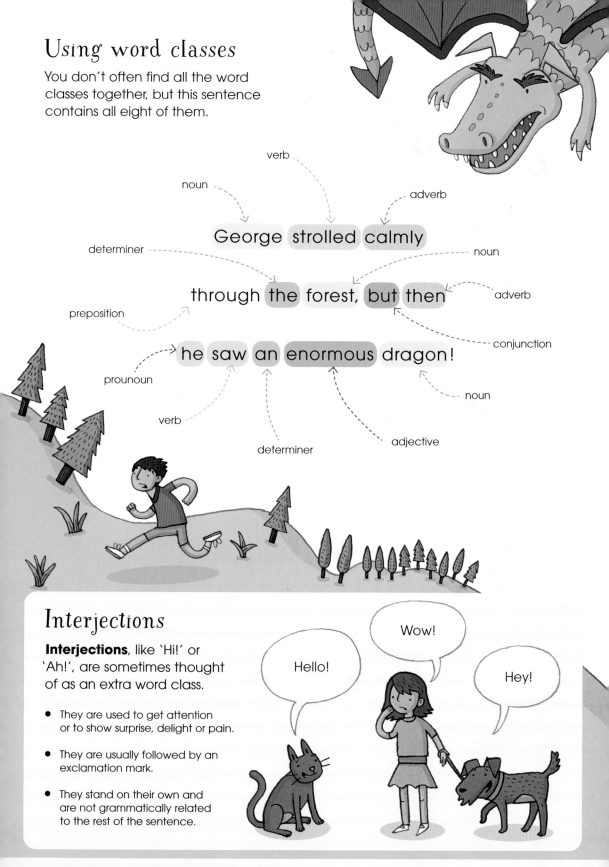

verb

noun

adverb

George strolled calmly

determiner

noun

through the forest, but then

preposition

adverb

conjunction

he saw an enormous dragon!

prounoun

verb

determiner

adjective

noun

Interjections

Interjections, like 'Hi!' or 'Ah!', are sometimes thought of as an extra word class.

- They are used to get attention or to show surprise, delight or pain.

- They are usually followed by an exclamation mark.

- They stand on their own and are not grammatically related to the rest of the sentence.

Hello!

Wow!

Hey!

Find out more about: **exclamation marks** (page 79).

Nouns

Nouns are words like 'Amy', 'tiger' or 'book' that tell you the name of a person, an animal or a thing. Ideas and feelings, like 'truth' and 'sadness', are nouns as well.

Most sentences contain at least one noun and a single sentence can have many nouns.

There are six nouns in this sentence.

Ryan had a dream that his rabbit was on a voyage through space in a rocket.

Proper nouns

Proper nouns tell you the name of one particular person, place or thing.

'Paris' is a proper noun because there's **only one** Paris.

Proper nouns always start with a **capital letter**.

I'm proper.

Paris

Superman   Christmas
Mexico   Elvis

Common nouns

You use a common noun when you're **not** talking about a particular, unique thing.

'Penguin' is a common noun because there are **lots** of penguins.

Common nouns **don't** have a capital letter unless they come at the beginning of a sentence.

I'm common.

penguin

cake   table
laughter   star

Proper nouns include...

- **places, countries, continents**

New York	Asia
Italy	Antarctica

- **oceans, mountains, rivers, lakes**

Pacific Ocean	Amazon River
Rocky Mountains	Lake Victoria

- **religious names**

Bible	Buddhism
Hinduism	Koran

- **historical names**

Roman Empire	Egyptians
World War I	Victorians

- **events and festivals**

Ramadan	Easter
New Year's Eve	Chanukah

Days, months and seasons

Days of the week and months of the year are proper nouns, so they start with a capital letter.

The four seasons are common nouns so they **don't** have a capital letter.

proper noun

Next Tuesday will be
the first day of spring.

common noun

Dad or dad?

Names of family members, such as 'dad' or 'granny', are usually common nouns, so they **don't** start with a capital letter.

How is your dad?

When a family name is used **instead** of someone's first name, it starts with a capital letter because it's being used as a proper noun.

Hello Dad!

Here comes Dad!

Concrete and abstract nouns

Nouns can be described as either concrete or abstract.

Concrete nouns represent things that **can** be seen, heard, touched, smelled or tasted. Most nouns are concrete.

computer	fish
shoulder	house

Abstract nouns represent things that **can't** be seen, heard, touched, smelled or tasted.

education	fear
jealousy	surprise

Singular and plural nouns

A noun can be singular and stand for just one thing, or it can be plural and represent more than one thing. Nouns usually change their spelling when they're plural.

Making plurals

- Most nouns simply gain an **s** to form the plural.

| bicycle | bicycle**s** |

- If a noun ends in **s**, **ss**, **x**, **zz**, **sh** or **ch**, you need to add **es**.

| bus | bus**es** |

| fox | fox**es** |

- If a noun ends in a **consonant** plus **y**, change the **y** to **ie** and add **s**.

| baby | bab**ies** |

- If a noun ends in **o**, you usually add **es**.

| hero | hero**es** |

- If a noun ends in **f** or **fe**, you often change the **f** or **fe** to **ves**.

| leaf | lea**ves** |

| knife | kni**ves** |

Tricky plurals

Some **irregular nouns** don't follow the usual rules for forming plurals.

| child | **children** |

| mouse | **mice** |

No change

A small group of nouns are exactly **the same** in the singular and plural forms.

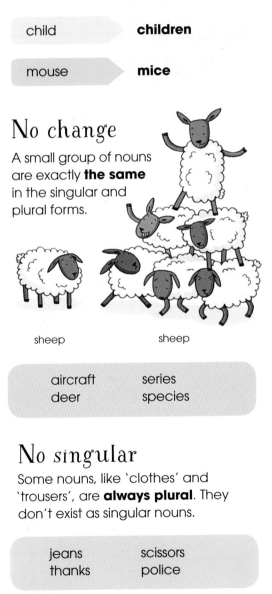

sheep   sheep

| aircraft | series |
| deer | species |

No singular

Some nouns, like 'clothes' and 'trousers', are **always plural**. They don't exist as singular nouns.

| jeans | scissors |
| thanks | police |

Uncountable nouns

Uncountable nouns, like 'luck' and 'butter', stand for things that can't be counted. This means they are **always singular**.

uncountable noun

This milk is fresh.

singular verb

Most abstract nouns can't be counted, and a small group of concrete nouns are uncountable too.

abstract	concrete
honesty	rice
happiness	bread
courage	flour
information	money

Collective nouns

Collective nouns, such as 'team' or 'flock', are **singular** even though they stand for many people or things.

collective noun

This bunch of flowers is beautiful.

singular verb

family	collection
group	class
choir	crowd

Using collective nouns

Some collective nouns can be tricky to use. It's not difficult to tell which of these two sentences is correct:

Your collection of buttons **is** amazing.

This is right.

Your collection of buttons **are** amazing.

This is wrong.

But it's much harder to decide which of these sounds right:

Our team **is** going to win.

Our team **are** going to win.

When a collective noun represents a group of people, it can feel more natural to use the plural form, so both the sentences above are correct.

Curious collective nouns

Collective nouns are often used for groups of animals. Some of them might surprise you!

- An army of ants
- A parliament of owls
- A pod of whales
- A pride of lions
- A crash of rhinos
- A dazzle of zebras

Find out about: **concrete and abstract nouns** (page 9).

Compound nouns

Compound nouns are made by putting **two or more words** together. They can be written as a single word, they can be linked by hyphens, or they can be two separate words.

- motorbike
- merry-go-round
- running shoes

Many compound nouns contain **two nouns**. The first noun tells you more about the second noun.

1st noun	2nd noun
pet	shop
bus	stop

Some compound nouns are made from a **noun** plus an **adjective** that describes the noun.

adjective	noun
full	moon
best	man

A few compound nouns contain a **noun** plus a **verb** that tells you more about the noun.

verb (present participle)	noun
swimming	pool
washing	machine

Using compound nouns

Compound nouns play the same role in a sentence as a one-word noun. This means you can use one or more adjectives in front of them.

Augustus wore a shiny black top hat.

- adjective
- adjective
- compound noun

Plural compound nouns

To form the plural of a compound noun, you need to add an **s** to one of the words. Usually, it's the last word that gains an **s**.

apple tree	apple tree**s**
merry-go-round	merry-go-round**s**

However, there are some exceptions that are important to remember.

mother-in-law	mother**s**-in-law
passer-by	passer**s**-by

If you're not sure how to spell a compound word, look it up in a dictionary. It will show you whether to use one word or two and if any hyphens are needed.

12   Find out about: **hyphens** (pages 97-98); **present participles** (page 25).

Test yourself on nouns

How much do you know about nouns? Use a pen and paper for these quizzes, then turn to page 130 to check your answers.

1 Spot the nouns

There are **20** nouns in this news report. Can you find them all? (Remember to watch out for compound nouns.)

On the evening of Monday 22 September, there was a break-in at the bank. The thieves tried to smash a window and then kicked down the door. A neighbour heard the noise and phoned the police, who arrived in less than ten minutes and made an arrest. The crime caused great alarm, but no money was stolen and there were no injuries. Two men were taken in a car to the police station.

2 Proper or common?

All the nouns in this email are shown in bold type. Can you spot **six** proper nouns and give them each a capital letter?

Hi **josh**

I hope you had a great **holiday** in **spain**. **rufus** really missed you. Let's meet next **wednesday** so you can tell me your **news**. We could have **lunch** at **peppers** at the **end** of your **street**.

See you next **week**.
moira
ps Send my **love** to your **dad**.

3 Singular to plural

Do you know the plurals of these nouns?

watch

foot

deer

tooth

potato

kiss

person

Pronouns

Pronouns are words like 'I', 'it' or 'they' that refer to a person, an animal or a thing without giving its name. Pronouns can also stand for something that's been mentioned or something that will be mentioned.

Using pronouns

A pronoun can stand for a **singular** or a **plural noun**.

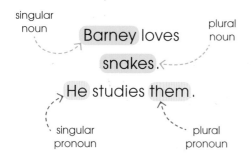

singular noun

plural noun

Barney loves snakes.

He studies them.

singular pronoun

plural pronoun

Pronouns can also refer to a **statement** or an **idea**.

Barney got lost in the jungle. It was very frightening.

pronoun standing for a statement

Why use pronouns?

When you use pronouns, you don't need to repeat the same words over and over again. This makes your writing much easier to read.

Barney saw the tiger and heard the tiger roar. Barney was in trouble. The fact that Barney was in trouble was very clear.

Barney saw the tiger and heard **it** roar. **It** was very clear that **he** was in trouble.

Changing pronouns

Pronouns change their form depending on whether they are the subject or the object in a sentence.

- The **subject** is the person or thing that does an action.

I saw the monkey.

----- pronoun as subject

- The **object** is the person or thing that has an action done to it.

The monkey saw me.

pronoun as object

- pronouns as **subject**:

singular	plural
I	we
you	you
he/she/it	they

- pronouns as **object**:

singular	plural
me	us
you	you
him/her/it	them

I or me?

Sometimes it can be hard to choose between the pronouns 'I' and 'me'.

Look at the sentences below. Which do you think is correct?

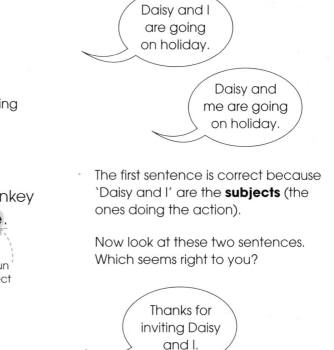

Daisy and I are going on holiday.

Daisy and me are going on holiday.

- The first sentence is correct because 'Daisy and I' are the **subjects** (the ones doing the action).

Now look at these two sentences. Which seems right to you?

Thanks for inviting Daisy and I.

Thanks for inviting Daisy and me.

The second sentence is correct because 'Daisy and me' are the **objects** (the ones having an action done to them).

To help choose the right pronoun, try simplifying the sentence so that you concentrate on **I** and **me**. First try saying: 'Thanks for inviting I.' Then try: 'Thanks for inviting me.' Which do you think sounds right?

Find out more about: **subjects and objects** (page 22).

Pronoun types

Pronouns can be used in several different ways. Here are some pronoun types you'll often come across.

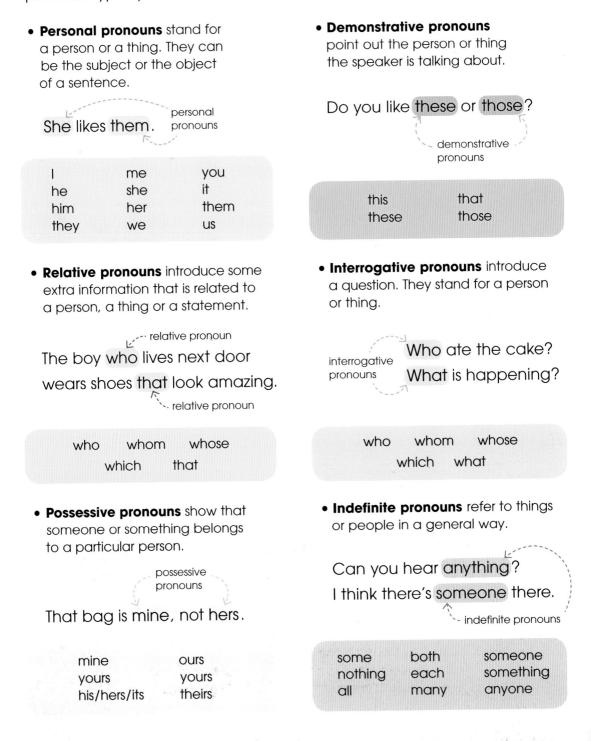

- **Personal pronouns** stand for a person or a thing. They can be the subject or the object of a sentence.

  She likes them. — personal pronouns

I	me	you
he	she	it
him	her	them
they	we	us

- **Relative pronouns** introduce some extra information that is related to a person, a thing or a statement.

  relative pronoun
  The boy who lives next door wears shoes that look amazing.
  relative pronoun

who	whom	whose
which	that	

- **Possessive pronouns** show that someone or something belongs to a particular person.

  possessive pronouns
  That bag is mine, not hers.

mine	ours
yours	yours
his/hers/its	theirs

- **Demonstrative pronouns** point out the person or thing the speaker is talking about.

  Do you like these or those?
  demonstrative pronouns

this	that
these	those

- **Interrogative pronouns** introduce a question. They stand for a person or thing.

  Who ate the cake?
  interrogative pronouns
  What is happening?

who	whom	whose
which	what	

- **Indefinite pronouns** refer to things or people in a general way.

  Can you hear anything?
  I think there's someone there.
  indefinite pronouns

some	both	someone
nothing	each	something
all	many	anyone

Test yourself on pronouns

Can you use pronouns correctly? Try these quizzes then check your answers on page 130.

1 Adding pronouns

Write out the text below, then fill in the gaps using the personal pronouns shown in the box. (You'll need to use some of them more than once.)

| I | you | he | she | it | we | they | me | him | us |

A strange creature was seen by Miss Kitty Keen as .... walked to school with a friend. Later, ... explained exactly what had happened. 'Finn and .... had just entered the park when a creature stepped out in front of .... . As .... can imagine, ... couldn't believe our eyes. Finn said .... gave .... a terrible shock.' Kitty went on to describe the creature. '.... looked like a large cat, but .... was covered in spots. .... told Finn .... was sure .... was a leopard, and .... agreed with .... . But when .... told our parents .... weren't convinced.'

2 I or me?

The pronouns 'I' and 'me' are used incorrectly in some of these sentences. Can you decide which ones are correct?

1.
Georgia is staying with Rosie and me.

2.
Why don't you come with Liam and I?

3.
Kamal and me went to the zoo.

4.
Bryony and me have known each other for years.

5.
Jack and I are best frends.

Adjectives

Adjectives are describing words, like 'hungry', 'tall' or 'interesting'. They give more information about a noun or a pronoun.

Often, the adjective goes **before** the **noun** it describes.

adjective   noun

I saw an enormous shark.

Sometimes, a verb separates the adjective from the noun or pronoun it describes. Then the adjective goes **after** the **verb**.

pronoun   adjective

It looked fierce.

verb

Adding adjectives

Writers often use two or more adjectives in a row.

Matty sails a beautiful old wooden boat.

adjectives   noun

noun

The sea was sparkling, cold and deep.

Adjectives add interest to your writing, but try not to use too many or they will lose their impact.

Comparatives and superlatives

You can use adjectives to compare people and things.

- To compare **two** people or things, use a **comparative**, such as 'taller'.

- To compare **three or more** people or things, use a **superlative**, such as 'the tallest'.

Mike's boat is fast.

⤷ adjective

Marco's boat is faster.

⤷ comparative

Meg's boat is the fastest.

superlative ⤷

Forming comparatives and superlatives

There are some simple rules for forming comparatives and superlatives.

- For the **comparative**, add **er** to the adjective.

- For the **superlative**, add **est** to the adjective and put the word **the** in front of it.

| loud | loud**er** | **the** loud**est** |

- If an adjective ends in **e**, add **r** for the **comparative** and **st** for the **superlative**.

| large | large**r** | **the** large**st** |

- For adjectives ending in **y**, change the **y** to **i** before adding **er** or **est**.

| happy | happ**ier** | **the** happ**iest** |

- Some adjectives **double** their final letter before adding **er** or **est**.

| big | big**ger** | **the** big**gest** |

- A few common adjectives **don't** follow the usual rules.

good	**better**	best
bad	**worse**	worst
little	**less**	least

More and the most

If an adjective has **more than two syllables**, you don't add 'er' or 'est'. Instead, you form the comparative and superlative by putting **more** and **the most** in front of the adjective.

Jo's ice cream is delicious.

    ↑
    `-- adjective

Jan's is more delicious.

    ↑
    `-- comparative

Mine is the most delicious.

    ↑
    `-- superlative

Watch out!

When you use a comparative that ends in 'er' or a superlative that ends in 'est', you should never add the words 'more' or 'the most'.

She is stronger. ✓

She is more stronger. ✗

He is the fastest. ✓

He is the most fastest. ✗

Less and the least

'less' and 'the least' can be used with adjectives of any length. They work in the same way as 'more' and 'the most'.

The monster is ugly.

The witch is less ugly.

The frog is the least ugly.

Fewer or less?

Many people feel confused about using 'fewer' or 'less'.

- You use **fewer** for things you **can** count.

  Evie has fewer dresses than Ella.

- You use **less** for something you **can't** count.

  Leo drinks less milk than Louis.

Find out about: **comparatives and superlatives** (page 19); **syllables** (page 119).

Test yourself on adjectives

You'll need a pen and paper to do these quizzes.
The answers are on page 130.

① Find the adjectives

This story contains **12** adjectives. Can you find them all?

The explorers felt tired, frightened and hungry, but they knew they had to go on. For hours, they hacked their way through the steamy jungle. Under their feet were thick, twisted creepers. Above their heads were tangled leaves and branches. They noticed a nasty smell coming from some invisible creature. Suddenly they heard a roar. It was very loud and deep. Would they ever escape from this terrible place?

② Fill in the gaps

There are **six** adjectives missing from these sentences. Choose the most suitable ones from the list below. (Warning: not all the words listed are adjectives!)

1. The .... ghost story made us feel .... .

2. Hanif was so .... he could see over the .... wall.

3. The cake was covered with .... icing and tasted very .... .

high	spooky	jump
pink	speedy	sweetly
terrify	tall	scared
bake	sweet	view

③ Making comparisons

Can you complete these animal comparisons by adding a comparative and a superlative? (The first one has been done for you.)

1. The caterpillar is long. The worm is **longer**. The snake is **the longest**.

2. The buffalo is heavy. The elephant is .... . The whale is ....

3. The worm is slimy. The snail is .... . The slug is ....

4. The dog is intelligent. The dolphin is .... The chimpanzee is ....

Verbs

Verbs are 'doing' or 'being' words, like 'run', 'eat' or 'live'. They change depending on the job they're doing in a sentence.

The verb is the most important part of any sentence. If you take it away, the sentence won't make sense.

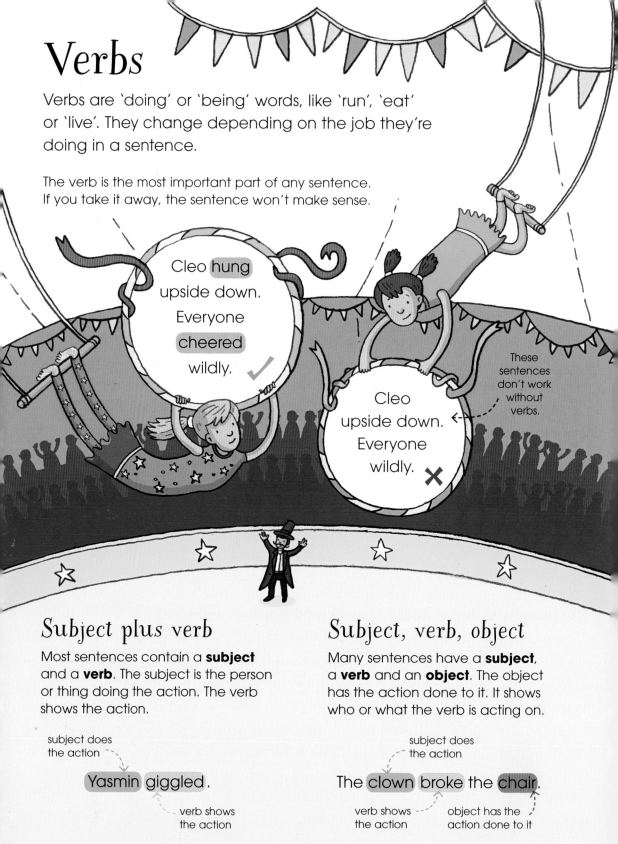

Cleo hung upside down. Everyone cheered wildly. ✓

Cleo upside down. Everyone wildly. ✗

These sentences don't work without verbs.

Subject plus verb

Most sentences contain a **subject** and a **verb**. The subject is the person or thing doing the action. The verb shows the action.

subject does the action

Yasmin giggled.

verb shows the action

Subject, verb, object

Many sentences have a **subject**, a **verb** and an **object**. The object has the action done to it. It shows who or what the verb is acting on.

subject does the action

The clown broke the chair.

verb shows the action

object has the action done to it

Transitive and intransitive verbs

- When a verb is used with a subject and an object it's called a **transitive** verb.

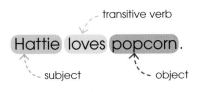

transitive verb

Hattie loves popcorn.

subject — object

Some transitive verbs:

hit	buy	make
give	collect	take

- When a verb has a subject but no object, it's an **intransitive** verb.

Ivan gasped.

subject — intransitive verb

Some intransitive verbs:

arrive	go	agree
sleep	stay	die

- Some verbs can be transitive **or** intransitive, depending on how they're used in a sentence.

intransitive verb has no object

Dev is driving. He is driving his car.

transitive verb has an object

Some verbs that can be transitive **or** intransitive:

eat	write	read
run	win	swim

Different subjects

The subject of a sentence can be either **singular** or **plural**. It can be in the **first** person, the **second** person or the **third** person.

	singular	plural
1st person	I run	we run
2nd person	you run	you run
3rd person	he/ she/ it runs	they run

Changing verbs

Verbs usually stay the same when their subject changes, except when the subject is the **third person singular** (he, she or it). Then the verb gains an **s**.

I drink. You drink.
We drink. They drink.

verb stays the same

She drinks.

third person singular

verb gains an **s**

Find out more about: **transitive and intransitive verbs** (pages 122-123); **changing verbs** (page 123).

23

Verb tenses

Verbs have different tenses to show the different times when an action happened. On the next few pages you can see how verbs change to form tenses.

Present simple

... shows an action that **often** happens or **usually** happens.

Jordan swims every day.
 ↑
 `--- present simple`

It is also used for **general statements**.

Monkeys like bananas.
 ↑
 `--- present simple`

To form the present simple, use the **infinitive** of the verb (see panel below), except when the subject of the verb is **third person singular** (he, she or it). Then you need to add a letter **s**.

I sing. You sing. He sings.
 ↑   ↑   ↑
`infinitive with`   `infinitive + s`
`no change`

What's the infinitive?

The infinitive is the basic form of a verb. It's the name a verb is known by and it often has the word 'to' in front of it. (For example, 'to play' or 'to run'.)

You use the infinitive to form the tenses of verbs, except for a few irregular verbs.

Past simple

... shows an action that happened and was **completed** in the past.

Amy walked home.
 ↑
 `past simple`

To form the past simple, you usually add **ed** or **d** to the infinitive of the verb.

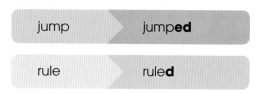

jump	jump**ed**
rule	rule**d**

Some **irregular verbs** change completely to make the past simple tense.

Here are some common examples:

infinitive	past simple
have	**had**
do	**did**
give	**gave**
go	**went**
see	**saw**

Present continuous

... shows an action that's **happening right now** in the present.

We are eating breakfast.

↑
‑‑‑ present continuous

It can also be used for **future** plans and arrangements.

Lily is coming tomorrow.

↑
‑‑ present continuous

To form the present continuous, use the **present simple** of the verb **be** ('am', 'are' or 'is') plus the **present participle** of the main verb in the sentence. (See panel below.)

Coco is sleeping.

↑
present simple
of the verb 'be'

present participle
of the main verb

What's the present participle?

The present participle is a verb form that's used to make some tenses. It's formed by adding '–ing' to the infinitive. For example, the verbs 'play' and 'fly' become 'playing' and 'flying'.

! Some verbs change their spelling in the present participle, so 'run' becomes 'running' and 'lie' becomes 'lying'.

Past continuous

... shows an action that happened in the past and **continued to another point** in the past. It often describes an action that was **interrupted** by something else.

‑‑ past continuous

Dan was playing the piano when he noticed the cat.

To form the past continuous, use the **past simple** of the verb **be** ('was' or 'were') plus the **present participle** of the main verb.

past simple of
the verb 'be'

The sun was shining when I woke up.

present participle
of the main verb

Find out more about: **actions in the future** (page 28-30).

Present perfect

... shows an action that happened in the past but is **still important in the present**.

Jess has finished her packing.

present perfect

To form the present perfect, use the **present simple** of the verb **have** ('have' or 'has') plus the **past participle** of the main verb. (See panel on this page.)

Jamal has baked a cake.

present simple of 'have'

past participle of the main verb

We have eaten it.

What's the past participle?

The past participle is a verb form that's used to make some tenses. It is formed in the same way as the past simple. For example, 'walk' becomes 'walked' and 'play' becomes 'played'.

! Some verbs have **irregular** past participles. Here are some common examples:

caught   begun
been   had   gone

Past perfect

... shows an action that happened in the past **before another action** in the past began.

past perfect

Holly had read the book before she saw the film.

To form the past perfect, use the **past simple** of the verb **have** ('had') plus the **past participle** of the main verb.

Janek was happy because he had scored a goal.

past simple of 'have'

past participle of the main verb

Present perfect continuous

... shows an action that began in the past and is **continuing up to the present**.

It has been raining for ages!

present perfect continuous

To form the present perfect continuous, use the **present perfect** of the verb **be** ('have been' or 'has been') plus the **present participle** of the main verb.

present perfect of 'be'

Sonia has been waiting since two o'clock.

present participle of the main verb

Be and have - auxiliary verbs

The verbs 'be' and 'have' are used with a main verb to form tenses. They are known as auxiliary verbs, or helping verbs, because they help the main verb.

Oli is walking to school.

auxiliary verb   main verb

Owen has waited for him.

Past perfect continuous

... shows an action that began in the past and **continued up to another point** in the past.

past perfect continuous

We had been talking for an hour when Al arrived.

To form the past perfect continuous, use the **past perfect** of the verb **be** ('had been') plus the **present participle** of the main verb.

Lucy felt tired after she had been jogging.

past perfect of 'be'   present participle of the main verb

Find out about: **present participles** (page 25).

Future simple

... shows an action that **will happen in the future**.

I will see Lola tomorrow.

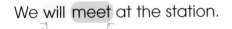
future simple

To form the future simple, you usually use **will** plus the **infinitive** of the main verb.

We will meet at the station.

'will' + infinitive of the main verb

Future continuous

... shows an action that will happen in the future and **will continue for a period of time**.

Next year, Jed will be playing for the Tigers.

future continuous

To form the future continuous, use **will be** plus the **present participle** of the main verb.

I will be supporting his team.

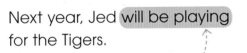
'will be' + present participle of the main verb

Future perfect

... shows an action that **will be completed** before a time in the future.

future perfect

Herbie will have moved house by the end of next week.

To form the future perfect, use **will have** plus the **past participle** of the main verb.

By next Saturday, he will have settled in happily.

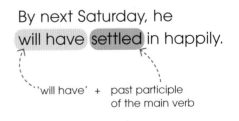
'will have' + past participle of the main verb

To make a **negative statement** about the future, simply change 'will' to **will not** or **won't**.

For example, 'Jed will not be playing for the Tigers next week.'

Future perfect continuous

... shows an action that **will continue up to a certain time** in the future.

In April, we will have been living here for ten years.

future perfect continuous

To form the future perfect continuous, use **will have been** plus the **present participle** of the main verb.

By lunchtime, Robbie will have been working on his sand castle for hours.

'will have been' + present participle of the main verb

Using 'will'

The verb **will** is used to form future tenses, but it has other uses too.

- It can show that someone is determined to do something.

  I will go to the match!

- It can be used for commands.

  Will you be quiet!

- It can be used for requests.

  Will you take Coco for a walk?

Using 'shall'

In the past, people often used **shall** instead of **will** in sentences about the future. They said, 'I shall see him tomorrow', instead of, 'I will see him tomorrow'.

Nowadays, 'shall' is used much less frequently. Most people only use it when they're asking a question or making a suggestion.

What shall we do now?

Shall I go first?

Find out about: **present participles** (page 25).

Talking about the future

There are several ways to talk or write about actions in the future.

- You can use the **future simple**.

  I will see you soon.

  ⌐- future simple

- You can use **going to** plus the **infinitive** of the main verb.

  We are going to play tennis.

  'going to' + infinitive of the main verb

- You can use the **present simple**.

  Zak arrives on Monday.

  ⌐- present simple

- You can use the **present continuous**.

  The play is starting soon.

  ⌐- present continuous

When you use the present simple or the present continuous, you usually need a word or phrase, such as 'soon' or 'on Monday', to show that the action will take place in the future.

Tenses at a glance

This chart shows how a regular verb like 'dance' changes to form different tenses:

present simple	I dance
present continuous	I am dancing
present perfect	I have danced
present perfect continuous	I have been dancing

past simple	I danced
past continuous	I was dancing
past perfect	I had danced
past perfect continuous	I had been dancing

future simple	I will dance
future continuous	I will be dancing
future perfect	I will have danced
future perfect continuous	I will have been dancing

Test yourself on tenses

Do you feel confident about using tenses? Use a pen and paper to do these quizzes, then check your answers on page 130.

 1 Into the past

Can you put the verbs in this message into the past simple tense? Write out the message, inserting the missing verbs. (All the verbs you need are in the box below.)

run   play   feel   sleep   find   swim

Yesterday, we went to the seaside. We .... in the sea, we .... along the beach, and we .... some beautiful shells. In the afternoon, we .... in the sand dunes. On the journey back, I .... very tired. I .... nearly all the way home!

Ashleigh McMorran

1 Geldart Row

London

SE1 12A

UK

2 Which tense?

All the verbs in the passage below are in bold text. Can you work out which tenses are being used?

Noah **loves** baseball. He **has been playing** since he was six years old. Last year he **played** for the Tigers. Now he **is playing** for the Lions, and soon he **will be joining** the Bears. Next year he **will play** in a national match. By then, he **will have played** five seasons of baseball.

Modal verbs

Modal verbs, like 'must', 'can' and 'should', are a type of auxiliary verb. They go in front of the main verb in a sentence and change its meaning.

Different meanings

Modal verbs can be used:

- to show that an action will happen in the **future**

  I will give Bobo a bath.

- to show that an action is **possible**

  I may give Bobo a bath.

- to show that an action is **needed** or **wanted**

  You must give Bobo a bath!

Some modal verbs:

can	shall
could	should
may	must
might	have to
will	need to
would	ought to

Asking permission

The modal verbs 'may', 'can', 'might' and 'could' can all be used to **ask** permission to do something. The modal verbs 'may' and 'can' are used to **give** permission.

May I have a cake?

You can go now.

In the past, children were taught that it wasn't polite to use the word 'can' to ask permission, but nowadays 'can' is widely used.

Using modal verbs

Modal verbs go **directly in front** of the main verb, which is used in the **infinitive**.

I might change my mind.

modal verb

infinitive of the main verb

The modal verbs **need, have** and **ought** are aways followed by the word **to** plus the **infinitive** of the main verb.

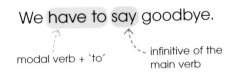

We have to say goodbye.

modal verb + 'to'

infinitive of the main verb

Phrasal verbs

A phrasal verb is a verb that gains new meaning when it's followed by a preposition or an adverb. For example, 'run into' and 'run away' are both phrasal verbs formed from the verb 'run'.

Making phrasal verbs

Phrasal verbs are usually made from two words, but a few have three.

give up	take after
find out	get away with
look forward to	throw away

Using phrasal verbs

Phrasal verbs can be **transitive** or **intransitive**.

Transitive phrasal verbs need an object in order to make sense.

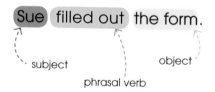

Sue filled out the form.

subject — phrasal verb — object

Intransitive phrasal verbs **don't** need an object.

The car broke down.

subject — phrasal verb without an object

Splitting phrasal verbs

Some transitive phrasal verbs can be split into two parts, so the object goes **between** the two parts of the verb.

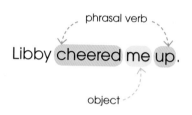

phrasal verb

Libby cheered me up.

object

Other phrasal verbs **can't** be split. Instead, the object goes **after** the phrasal verb.

Toby looks after two rabbits.

phrasal verb — object

Find out more about: **phrasal verbs** (page 122); **transitive and intransitive verbs** (page 23).

Active and passive

Verbs are generally used in the active voice, as in the sentence 'I dropped the mug.' But they can also be used in the passive voice, as in 'The mug was dropped.' When you use the passive voice, your writing sounds less personal and less direct.

Active and passive voices

When a sentence is in the **active** voice, the **subject does the action**.

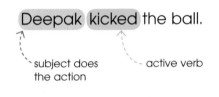

Deepak kicked the ball.

subject does the action — active verb

When a sentence is in the **passive** voice, the **subject is acted on**.

The ball was kicked.

subject is acted on — passive verb

Forming passive sentences

To form a passive sentence, you use the verb **be** with the **past participle** of the main verb.

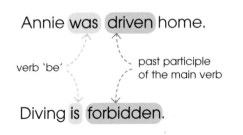

Annie was driven home.

verb 'be' — past participle of the main verb

Diving is forbidden.

Using passive sentences

You use the passive voice when:

- you don't know who did the action

  The cakes have been eaten.

- you're interested in the action, rather than the person who did it

  The road has been repaired.

- you don't want to say who did something

  Mistakes were made.

- you want to give an instruction, without being too bossy or direct

DOGS MUST BE KEPT ON A LEAD

Find out about: **subjects** (page 22); **past participles** (page 26).

Test yourself on verbs

Can you recognize a passive sentence, and do you know how to use modal verbs? The answers to these quizzes are on page 131.

 Active or passive?

Which sentences are active and which are passive?

1.
Henry was eating an apple.

2.
The egg was laid by a pigeon.

3.
The tower has collapsed.

4.
Tina opened her present.

5.
The painting was stolen.

2 Adding modal verbs

Can you find a modal verb to fill each of the gaps? Write out your sentences using verbs from the list below.

> should   must   would   ought   have

1. That bull is heading for us! We .... run!
2. The bus is usually on time. It .... to be here very soon.
3. If you're feeling tired, you .... go to bed.
4. What .... you like to do today?
5. There's no alternative. We .... to obey the law.

Adverbs

Adverbs are words like 'quietly' or 'sleepily' that give more information about another word. They usually work with verbs, but they can also be used with adjectives or with other adverbs.

When, where, how?

An adverb can work with a verb to tell you **when**, **where** or **how** something happens.

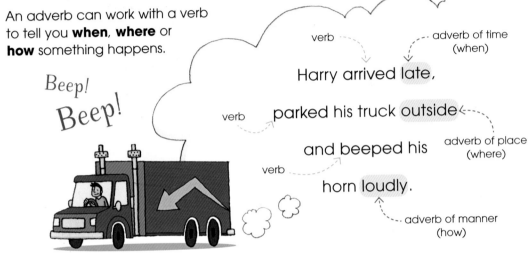

Beep!
Beep!

verb ---- adverb of time (when)

Harry arrived late,

verb ---- parked his truck outside ---- adverb of place (where)

and beeped his

verb ---- horn loudly.

adverb of manner (how)

Time

Adverbs of time answer the questions 'When?', 'How often?' or 'For how long?'

When? Let's meet **soon**.

How often? I **always** walk home.

For how long? They talked **briefly**.

Some adverbs of time:

tomorrow	daily
now	sometimes

Place

Adverbs of place answer the questions 'Where?' or 'In what direction?'

Where? I've looked **everywhere**.

In what direction? Ed shuffled **sideways**.

Some adverbs of place:

indoors	near
abroad	nowhere
there	forwards

Manner

Adverbs of manner answer the question 'How was it done?'

Caspar cycled **rapidly**, **wildly** and **dangerously**.

They are usually formed by adding the letters **ly** to an **adjective**.

slow	slow**ly**
beautiful	beautiful**ly**

If an adjective ends in **y**, change the y to **i** before adding **ly**.

happy	happ**i**ly
easy	eas**i**ly

Irregular adverbs

Not all adverbs of manner are formed by adding **ly**. Here are some irregular adverbs:

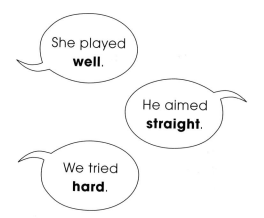

She played **well**.

He aimed **straight**.

We tried **hard**.

Adverb or adjective?

Some words, like 'hard', 'straight' and 'early', can be either an adverb **or** an adjective, depending on whether they're working with a verb or a noun.

Beth **drives** ···· verb

fast. ····· adverb

She has a

fast car.

adjective ···· noun

- If the word answers the questions 'How?', 'When?', 'Where?' or 'Why?', it's an **adverb**.

- If the word answers the question 'What is it like?', it's an **adjective**.

Watch out!

A few adjectives, like 'silly' and 'ghostly', already end in **ly**, so you can't add another **ly** to turn them into an adverb. Instead, you need to use them in a short phrase.

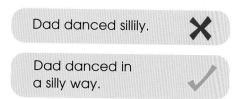

Dad danced sillily. ✗

Dad danced in a silly way. ✓

Find out about: **adjectives** (pages 18-20).

Adverbs of degree

Adverbs of degree answer the question 'How much?' They work with other words to make them stronger or weaker.

Donkeys run quite fast.

adverb of degree

Antelopes run extremely fast.

adverb of degree

Cheetahs run incredibly fast.

adverb of degree

Some more adverbs of degree:

fairly	very
rather	really
too	hardly

Using adverbs of degree

Adverbs of degree can be used with an **adverb**, an **adjective** or a **verb**.

Horace sings very loudly.

adverb of degree — adverb

Sophie is rather bossy.

adverb of degree — adjective

I have almost finished.

adverb of degree — verb

Too many adverbs

Some people use adverbs of degree to give extra emphasis to their writing, but these adverbs need to be used with care. If you use too many, they will reduce the impact of your words.

Dearest Maisie,

I'm having a **simply** brilliant holiday. The sun is **amazingly** hot, the sea is **gloriously** blue, and the food is **perfectly** delicious. I'm **fantastically** glad to be here, but of course I'm missing you **dreadfully**.

With **absolutely** heaps of love,

Rupert xxxxxx

Test yourself on adverbs

How much do you know about adverbs? Use a pen and paper to do these quizzes, then turn to page 131 to see the answers.

① Spot the adverbs

Five of these words are adverbs. Can you identify them?

thin   backwards

truck   understand

mysterious

easily   very   vanish

yesterday   speedy

somewhere

② Time, place, manner and degree

This list of adverbs contains **two** adverbs of time, **two** adverbs of place, **two** adverbs of manner and **two** adverbs of degree.

Can you sort the adverbs into **four** groups?

- slowly
- quite
- early
- here
- indoors
- never
- really
- carefully

③ Fill in the gaps

Choose the most suitable adverbs from the list below to complete these sentences. But beware – not all the words in the list are adverbs!

everywhere
violent
hardly
late
passionately
hopeless
fast
hurried
straight
extremely

1. Mia aimed .... for the bullseye.

2. Yusuf .... made any mistakes.

3. Finlay looked .... for his phone.

4. Erin ran as .... as she could, but she still arrived .... for school.

5. Chimpanzees are .... intelligent.

6. Jason loves Juliet .... .

Prepositions

Prepositions are words like 'on', 'through' and 'during'. They show where something is in relation to something else, or when something happened.

Prepositions are always followed by a noun, a pronoun or a noun phrase (a group of words containing a noun).

Lauren went on the roller coaster.

She waved as she raced past us.

Alfie felt ill after the wild ride.

Place, time, movement

Prepositions can show **place**, **time** or **movement**.

Maya runs in the park.

↑ preposition of place

She runs before breakfast.

↑ preposition of time

She runs across the grass.

↑ preposition of movement

place	time	movement
at	at	through
on	on	past
in	in	into
under	during	over

Simple or complex

Prepositions can be simple or complex. **Simple** prepositions are **single words** like 'on' or 'past'.

Complex prepositions are made from **two or more words** that act as a single unit. Here are some examples:

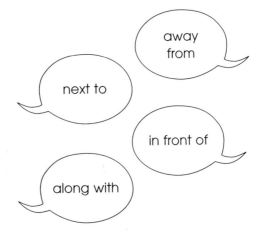

away from

next to

in front of

along with

Test yourself on prepositions

Do you understand how prepositions work? Write down your answers to these quizzes, then turn to page 131 to see how well you've done.

1 Spot the prepositions

There are **nine** prepositions in this paragraph. Can you find them all?

Alice clambered over the wall, wriggled through some bushes and found herself in the garden. She raced across the lawn, hurtled round the pond and swerved past the statue. Then she ran up the path leading to the house, and knocked loudly on Jasper's window.

2 Time, place or movement?

Can you spot **four** prepositions of place, **three** prepositions of time and **one** preposition of movement in this passage? (The prepositions 'on', 'at' and 'in' can show either place or time. The preposition 'past' can show time or movement.)

We met at the station on Monday night. The train was due to arrive in ten minutes, but it was delayed. First, we sat in the café. Then we stood on the platform and gazed at the view. Many trains went racing past us, but none of them stopped. It was past midnight when we finally caught our train.

Conjunctions

Conjunctions are words like 'and', 'because' or 'but'. They provide a link between different words and are sometimes known as connectives.

Conjunctions can be used to link two **words** or to connect two **parts** of a sentence.

The witches added frogs and spiders, but their spell still didn't work.

Co-ordinating conjunctions

Co-ordinating conjunctions, like 'and', 'but' and 'or', link two statements that can each stand on their own and are each **equally important**.

These two statements are equally important.

Goblins are noisy, but fairies are quiet.

co-ordinating conjunction

Some co-ordinating conjunctions:

and	nor
yet	or
but	so

Subordinating conjunctions

Subordinating conjunctions link two statements that are **not** equally important. One statement is the **main clause** and the other is the **subordinate clause**.

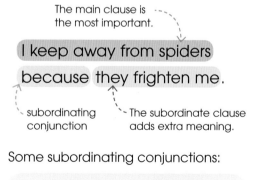

The main clause is the most important.

I keep away from spiders because they frighten me.

subordinating conjunction

The subordinate clause adds extra meaning.

Some subordinating conjunctions:

although	because
if	unless
when	where

Find out about: **main clauses and subordinate clauses** (page 50).

Using subordinating conjunctions

You can use a subordinating conjunction in two different positions.

- It can be placed **between** two statements:

The dragon slept soundly **although** the knight kept sneezing.

conjunction

subordinate clause

main clause

- Or it can come at the **start** of a sentence:

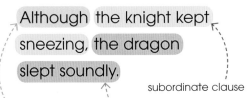

Although the knight kept sneezing, the dragon slept soundly.

subordinate clause

conjunction

main clause

When you change the position of a conjunction, you emphasize a different part of the sentence.

Comma alert!

When you use a conjunction at the **start** of a sentence, it must be followed by two statements divided by a **comma**.

conjunction — first statement

If you want to visit the castle , you must cross the bridge .

second statement

Add a comma after the first statement.

conjunction — first statement

Unless you are very careful , you will fall .

second statement

Add a comma after the first statement.

Starting sentences

In the past, people often insisted that a sentence should never start with 'And' or 'But'. Nowadays, however, these rules are not so strictly followed. Many good writers use the words 'And' or 'But' to introduce a sentence.

Find out more about: **commas with conjunctions** (page 83).

Determiners

Determiners are words like 'a', 'the' and 'some'. You use a determiner to make it clear which person, animal or thing you're talking about.

Articles

The most common determiners are 'a', 'an' and 'the'. These three words are known as articles. Articles go in front of a **noun** or in front of the **adjectives** belonging to a noun.

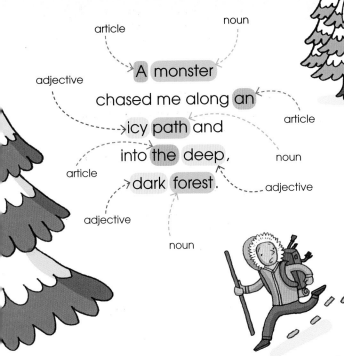

article — A noun — monster

adjective — chased me along an — article

icy path and

into the deep, — noun

article — dark forest. — adjective

adjective

noun

Definite articles

The word 'the' is a **definite article**. It refers to a **particular** thing that is already known or has been mentioned before.

The monster roared.

definite article

Indefinite articles

The words 'a' and 'an' are **indefinite articles**. They refer to something that is **not** specific or known.

A bird squawked.

indefinite article

'A' or 'an'?

In some sentences, the word 'an' is used instead of 'a' to make speaking easier.

- You use 'a' when the next word begins with a **consonant**. (A consonant is any letter of the alphabet except a, e, i, o and u, which are all **vowels**.)

- You use 'an' when the next word starts with a **vowel** sound.

word starting with a consonant

The monkey ate **a** banana,

an apple and **an** orange.

words starting with a vowel

Watch out!

Some words beginning with the letter **h** don't start with a consonant you can hear, so you need to use 'an' instead of 'a'.

- an hour
- an honest man

Some words beginning with the letter **u** actually start with the consonant sound **y**. So you need to use 'a' instead of 'an'.

- a unicorn
- a united team

Different determiners

Determiners can be used in several ways. Here are some different types.

- **Possessives** show which person or thing something or someone belongs to.

-- possessive

I've found my ticket.

Have you found your bag?

possessive --

my	her	his	its
your	our	their	

- **Demonstratives** show which person or thing is being talked or written about.

-- demonstrative

Rose likes this dress but

Ruby prefers that one.

demonstrative --

this	that
these	those

- **Interrogatives** are used to ask questions about a person or thing.

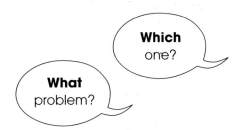

Which one?

What problem?

Find out more about: **vowels and consonants** (pages 116-117).

Showing numbers

Some determiners show numbers, amounts or quantities.

Quantifiers show the **amount** of people, animals or things.

Matt has eaten half the cakes.

quantifier

some	double	much
both	most	little
all	any	many

Cardinal numbers show the **number** of people, animals or things.

cardinal number

I saw four birds all sitting on one branch.

cardinal number

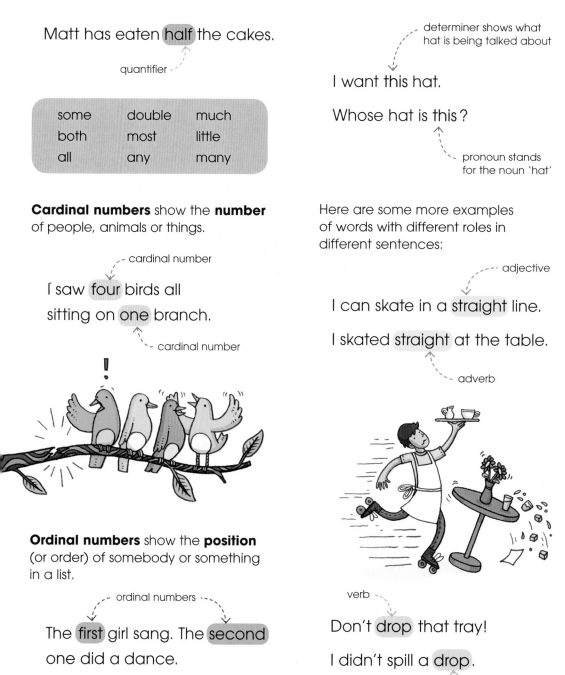

Ordinal numbers show the **position** (or order) of somebody or something in a list.

ordinal numbers

The first girl sang. The second one did a dance.

Which word class?

The same words can play **different roles** in different sentences.

For example, the word 'this' can be a determiner **or** a pronoun.

determiner shows what hat is being talked about

I want this hat.

Whose hat is this?

pronoun stands for the noun 'hat'

Here are some more examples of words with different roles in different sentences:

adjective

I can skate in a straight line.

I skated straight at the table.

adverb

verb

Don't drop that tray!

I didn't spill a drop.

noun

Test yourself on conjunctions and determiners

Use a pen and paper to do these quizzes. Then turn to page 131 to check your answers.

① Adding conjunctions

There are **five** conjunctions missing from this passage. Can you write it out using the words in the box to fill the gaps?

until
because
where
and
but

We climbed the hill .... we wanted to see the view, ... the walk was very tiring. We kept going .... we got to the top. At last we reached a place .... we could see the next valley. I took a quick look .... climbed down the hill again.

② Which determiner?

Can you pick the right determiner for each of these sentences? Use the words from the list below to fill the gaps.

no   many   the   my   any   an

1. Hardly .... children turned up for the party.
2. I liked the film, but I haven't read .... book.
3. Hurry up! There's .... time to waste.
4. Have you seen .... coat? I can only find yours.
5. Is that a monkey or .... ape?
6. I can't decide what to eat. There are too .... choices.

Looking at sentences

A sentence is a group of words that contains at least one verb and makes sense on its own. All sentences start with a capital letter. They can end with a full stop, a question mark or an exclamation mark.

Statements

Most sentences are statements that tell you something. Statements always end with a **full stop**.

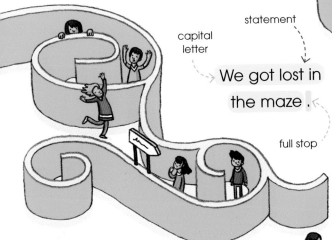

statement

capital letter

We got lost in the maze .

full stop

Questions

Sentences that ask a question end with a **question mark**. They often contain the verbs 'be', 'do' or 'can'.

- **Is** there a map?
- **Do** you know where we are?
- **Can** we get out of here?

Many questions start with the question words 'why', 'when', 'where', 'how', 'what' or 'who'.

- **Where** is Lucas?
- **What** is he doing?

Exclamations

Exclamations show surprise, disagreement, pleasure or some other strong emotion. They end with an **exclamation mark**.

Exclamations often start with the words 'what' or 'how'.

- **What** a confusing maze this is!
- **How** tall the hedges are!

Instructions and commands

Instructions and commands tell you to do something. **Instructions** usually end with a **full stop**.

Please leave quietly.

Commands demand your attention, so they end with an **exclamation mark**.

Stop talking now!

Sentence fragments

Sentence fragments **don't** contain a verb so they're not proper sentences. Sentence fragments can be:

- One-word questions

Why?   How?

- One-word responses

Yes.   No.

- Short exclamations

Oh!   Hey!

- Greetings

Happy Birthday!   Good morning!

Long or short

- Sentences can be very short:

Gracie threw the ball.

- But they can also be long:

My little sister Gracie gathered all her strength and threw the ball as hard as she could over the high garden wall.

Short sentences are much easier to read than long, complicated ones, but too many short sentences in a row can make your writing sound jerky.

Sentences, clauses and phrases

Sentences are made up of clauses and phrases. A **clause** is a group of words built around a verb. A **phrase** is a group of words that adds extra information to a sentence. Many phrases don't contain verbs.

clause

Gracie threw the ball over the wall.

phrase

You can find out more about clauses and phrases on the next few pages.

Find out more about: **clauses** (pages 50-52); **phrases** (pages 54-56).

Clauses and sentences

A clause is a group of words built around a verb. All sentences contain at least one clause, and sentences are often made from two or more clauses.

Different clauses

Clauses can be **main** or **subordinate**. Every sentence has one or more main clauses, but only some sentences contain subordinate clauses.

Main clauses

Main clauses **make sense on their own**. They are sometimes known as independent clauses.

Josie saw an alien.

main clause built around the verb 'saw'

Subordinate clauses

Subordinate clauses **add extra information** to a main clause. They are sometimes called dependent clauses because they can't usually stand alone.

Main clause can stand as a statement on its own.

Josie saw an alien that was bright purple.

Subordinate clause adds extra information but doesn't make sense on its own.

Spotting subordinate clauses

Subordinate clauses are introduced by **subordinating conjunctions**. Here are some common ones to look out for:

which	that
because	although
when	where
if	while
unless	until

Find out more about: **subordinating conjunctions** (pages 42-43).

Simple sentences

Simple sentences have just **one main clause**. They are often short, but some simple sentences can be surprisingly long.

The alien smiled.

Both these simple sentences have just one main clause built around the verb 'smiled'.

The purple alien with eyes on stalks smiled at Josie in a shy yet friendly way.

Compound sentences

Compound sentences have **two or more main clauses** linked by a co-ordinating conjunction, such as 'and', 'or', 'so' or 'but'.

first main clause

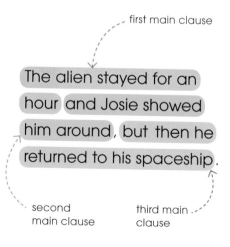

The alien stayed for an hour and Josie showed him around, but then he returned to his spaceship.

second main clause

third main clause

Each of the clauses in a compound sentence can stand as a statement on its own.

Complex sentences

Complex sentences contain a main clause **plus** one or more subordinate clauses.

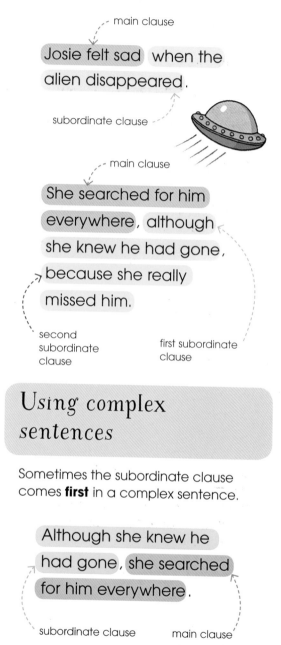

main clause

Josie felt sad when the alien disappeared.

subordinate clause

main clause

She searched for him everywhere, although she knew he had gone, because she really missed him.

second subordinate clause

first subordinate clause

Using complex sentences

Sometimes the subordinate clause comes **first** in a complex sentence.

Although she knew he had gone, she searched for him everywhere.

subordinate clause

main clause

When the subordinate clause comes before the main clause, you need to separate the clauses with a **comma**.

Find out more about: **co-ordinating conjunctions** (page 42).

Relative clauses

A relative clause is a type of subordinate clause. It does the same job as an adjective, giving more information about a noun or a pronoun.

Using relative clauses

Relative clauses start with a **relative pronoun**, such as 'who', 'which', 'that', 'whom' or 'whose'.

- A relative clause can come at the **end** of a sentence.

This is the boy who lives next door.

main clause   relative clause

- Or it can come in the **middle** of a sentence.

The boy who lives next door is waving at me.

main clause   relative clause

Cutting 'that'

People often cut the pronoun 'that' from the start of a relative clause:

 I've lost the book **that** I was reading.

✓ I've lost the book I was reading.

The sentence without 'that' is still grammatically correct.

Who or whom?

It's grammatically correct to use the word 'whom' when it's the **object** of a clause. However, many people think it sounds very old-fashioned.

There is the girl whom we met earlier.

'whom' is the object of the verb 'met'.

I don't mind whom you invite.

'whom' is the object of the verb 'invite'.

In some cases, it's possible to rephrase a sentence so the word 'whom' is left out. In others, people choose to use the word 'who' because it sounds less formal than 'whom'.

There is the girl we met earlier.

I don't mind who you invite.

Test yourself on sentences and clauses

These quizzes will test your knowledge of sentences and clauses. The answers are on page 131.

1 Simple, compound or complex?

This passage contains **two simple sentences** (sentences with just one main clause), **two compound sentences** (sentences with two or more main clauses) and **two complex sentences** (sentences with a main clause and one or more subordinate clauses). Can you find them all?

> Eric loved fishing. He went fishing every day, but he never caught anything. Although he waited patiently for hours, nothing ever happened. Then one day he felt a pull on his fishing line. He heaved with all his strength and he pulled out a boot! When Eric realized what he had caught, he was very disappointed.

2 Main clause or subordinate clause?

Each of these sentences has one main clause and one subordinate clause. Can you find the subordinate clause in each sentence?

1. Meera, who had trained for months, won the race.
2. We stayed at home because it was raining.
3. We were happy until Bernard came to stay.
4. If the rain stops, we will go out.
5. We've finished the game that we were playing.
6. Although Kerry tried hard, she didn't win any prizes.

Looking at phrases

A phrase is a group of two or more words that acts as a single unit, adding more information to a sentence. Many phrases don't contain a verb. They can take the place of a noun, an adjective or an adverb.

Noun phrases

... do the same job as **nouns** in a sentence. They can be the **subject** or the **object** of a sentence.

noun phrase as subject - built around the noun 'musicians'

Some talented musicians are playing shiny new instruments.

noun phrase as object - built around the noun 'instruments'

Adjective phrases

... do the same job as **adjectives**. They add extra information to an adjective.

The tuba makes a loud but musical sound.

adjective phrase adding to the adjective 'loud'

Adverb phrases

... do the same job as **adverbs**, giving more information about a verb.

The drummer plays extremely energetically.

adverb phrase adding to the verb 'plays'

Preposition phrases

... show **where** something is, **when** something happened, or **how** something relates to other things. They always start with a **preposition**.

Preposition phrases usually act like an **adverb,** giving more information about a verb.

Dylan lost his music ~~before the concert~~.

preposition phrase adding to the verb 'lost'

Sometimes, a preposition phrase can act as an **adjective**, giving more information about a noun.

The man in the back row has dropped his trumpet.

preposition phrase adding to the noun 'man'

Fronted or embedded?

Phrases often come at the **end** of a sentence, but they can also be used in the **front** or the **middle** of a sentence.

When you use a phrase, it's up to you to decide which position works best.

- A **fronted** phrase is placed at the front of a sentence. It is usually followed by a **comma**.

fronted phrase

Behind the stage, the band was waiting to play a song.

- An **embedded** phrase is placed in the middle of a sentence with **no** added commas.

The band was waiting behind the stage to play a song.

embedded phrase

Misplaced phrases

Sometimes a phrase can be in the wrong position in a sentence. This can make the sentence unclear or even ridiculous.

The boy spotted a dolphin with binoculars.

This phrase seems to refer to the noun 'dolphin'.

If the meaning of your sentence isn't clear, you need to move the phrase closer to the word that it relates to.

The boy with binoculars spotted a dolphin.

This phrase clearly refers to the noun 'boy'

Long phrase alert!

When you use a long phrase, make sure it doesn't **separate** the subject from its verb. If a subject is a long way from its verb, the sentence can be very hard to read.

subject

Poppy, along with her brothers, her Auntie Lizzie and her puppy, Yoyo, headed for the beach.

verb

This phrase separates the subject from its verb.

As soon as you put the verb next to the subject, the meaning of the sentence becomes much clearer.

subject   verb

Poppy headed for the beach, along with her brothers, her Auntie Lizzie and her puppy, Yoyo.

This phrase clearly adds information to the subject.

Test yourself on clauses and phrases

Do you feel confident about using clauses and phrases? Try these quizzes, then check your answers on page 132.

1 Phrase or clause?

In this passage, the phrases and subordinate clauses are shown in bold type. Can you find **seven** phrases and **four** subordinate clauses? (Remember – clauses always contain a verb.)

The travellers trudged wearily **across the desert**. They kept on walking **until they could hardly move**. **By the end of the day** they had to stop to rest **every few minutes**. **Some of them** dreamed of home **as they walked**. Others peered **into the distance**. They hoped to see a village **where they could sleep**. But there was sand **wherever they looked**. **In the end**, they gave up. They settled down to sleep **under the stars**.

2 Adding phrases

Can you complete this story? Write it out on a piece of paper, choosing the right phrases to fill the gaps.

.... Molly has a .... pet. He is called Cedric and he lives .... , Molly took Cedric .... and he escaped! He slithered .... and .... . Mrs Boggins, ... , spotted Cedric and screamed .... . Molly had to promise that Cedric would not be allowed out .... .

into the garden
our next-door neighbour
across the grass
in panic
very unusual
under the fence
any more
in a cardboard box
Last Monday
My little sister

Direct and reported speech

When you write down what a person said, you can use direct speech or reported speech. For direct speech, you write down someone's exact words. For reported speech, you report what was said in your own words.

direct speech

'I feel sick,' said Jake.

Zadie said he should cheer up.

reported speech

For direct speech...

- Put the exact words that were spoken inside quotation marks.

- Add a simple clause, such as 'said Jake', to explain who's speaking.

- Use a comma, a question mark or an exclamation mark to separate the speech from the clause explaining who's speaking.

quotation marks contain the speech

'I want to go home,'

said Jake.

clause explains who's speaking

comma marks the end of the speech

For reported speech...

- Start the sentence with a simple clause introducing the person who's speaking.

- Use your own words to report what was said and **don't** use quotation marks.

- Use a full stop to mark the end of the reported speech.

clause introduces the person who's speaking

Jake said he wanted to go home.

full stop marks the end of the speech

Find out more about: **quotation marks** (pages 86-88); **clauses** (pages 50-52).

Tenses in speech

- In **direct speech**, the clause explaining who's speaking is usually in the past tense. (For example, 'he said'.) But the speech inside quotation marks can be in the past, the present or the future.

'We are lost,' said Emily.

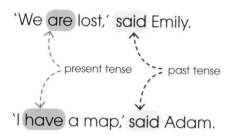

present tense   past tense

'I have a map,' said Adam.

- In **reported speech**, you are reporting something that was said in the past, so the speech is **always** in a past tense.

Emily said they were lost.

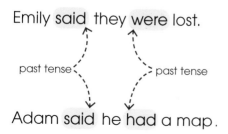

past tense   past tense

Adam said he had a map.

Tenses in reported speech

For reported speech, you need to go back **one more step** from the tense that was used in direct speech.

For example, if the speaker uses the past simple in direct speech, you need to use the past perfect in reported speech:

- direct speech

  'I saw a stingray,' said Isaac.

  past simple

- reported speech

  Isaac said he had seen a stingray.

  past perfect

This chart will help you change tenses from direct speech to reported speech:

direct speech	reported speech
smiles *present simple*	smiled *past simple*
is smiling *present continuous*	was smiling *past continuous*
has smiled *present perfect*	had smiled *past perfect*
smiled *past simple*	had smiled *past perfect*
had smiled *past perfect*	had smiled *past perfect*

Find out more about: **tenses** (pages 24-30).

Reporting speech about the future

If a speech is about something that will happen in the future, you need to change the word **will** to **would**.

- direct speech

'I will catch a fish,' said Fred.

- reported speech

Fred said he would catch a fish.

will always changes to **would** in reported speech about the future.

will dance	**would** dance
will be dancing	**would** be dancing
will have danced	**would** have danced
will have been dancing	**would** have been dancing

Can to could

When you put **can** and **can't** into reported speech, they change to **could** and **couldn't**.

- direct speech

'I can swim, but Mona can't,' said Matt.

- reported speech

Matt said he could swim but Mona couldn't.

Reporting general statements

Some general statements, like 'seals eat fish', always have their verb in the **present** tense. This means they **don't** change tense in reported speech.

- direct speech

'Blue whales are enormous,' said Melissa.

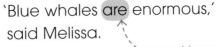
~ present tense

- reported speech

Melissa said that blue whales are enormous.

verb stays in the present tense

 Find out more about: **direct and reported speech** (pages 58-59).

Reporting questions

When you put a question into reported speech, you need to make several changes:

- Remove the question mark
- Change the tense of the verb
- Change the position of the verb in the sentence

'Where is the beach?' asked Sam.	Sam asked where the beach **was**.

direct speech   reported speech

For questions that **don't** start with a question word (such as what, where, who or why), you need to add **if** or **whether**.

- Use **if** for a **simple question** with no alternatives.

'Is Jay coming?' asked Bella.	Bella asked **if** Jay was coming.

direct speech   reported speech

- Use **whether** for a question with **two or more** alternatives to choose between.

'Is Jay coming or not?' asked Bella.	Bella asked **whether** Jay was coming **or** not.

direct speech   reported speech

Reporting commands or advice

When you report commands or advice, you need to make these changes:

- Put the word 'to' in front of the verb
- Change the verb 'said' to a different verb, such as 'told', 'ordered', 'warned' or 'advised'
- Remove any exclamation marks from the end of the speech

'Dive straight in!' Katie said.	Katie ordered Kai **to** dive straight in.

direct speech   reported speech

'Watch out for jellyfish,' Joel said.	Joel advised Anna **to** watch out for jellyfish.

direct speech   reported speech

Changing people

When you use reported speech, you need to think about who is doing the speaking and who is being spoken to. Then you can change the relevant words.

- direct speech

'I like your hat,' Tilly told Tom.

- reported speech

'she' stands for 'Tilly'

Tilly told Tom **she** liked **his** hat.

'his' stands for 'Tom's'

If the person doing the speaking and the person being spoken to are both male or both female, you may need to repeat one of their names to make your meaning clear.

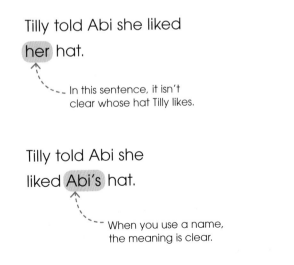

Tilly told Abi she liked **her** hat.

In this sentence, it isn't clear whose hat Tilly likes.

Tilly told Abi she liked **Abi's** hat.

When you use a name, the meaning is clear.

Changing times and places

When you move from direct speech to reported speech, you usually need to change the **times** and **places** mentioned. Sometimes, you may need to change the **verb** as well.

- direct speech

'Come back here tomorrow,' said Mr Plum.

- reported speech

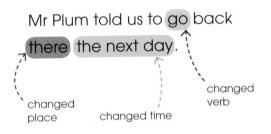

Mr Plum told us to **go** back **there** the next day.

changed place

changed time

changed verb

Here are some common words and phrases that change when they're used in reported speech:

today	that day
yesterday	the day before
here	there
now	then
this	that

Test yourself on direct and reported speech

Use a pen and paper to do these quizzes, then turn
to page 132 to check your answers.

 Direct to reported speech

Can you write out these sentences in reported speech?

1. 'It's too late,' I said.　　　　　　　I said it .... .

2. 'I did it earlier,' Isabella said.　　　Isabella said that .... .

3. 'Watch out!' said Mum.　　　　　　Mum told us .... .

4. 'I will do it tomorrow,' Dad said.　　Dad said that .... .

5. 'Can I sit down?' Will asked.　　　　Will asked .... .

2 Making it direct

These five sentences are in reported speech. Can you rewrite them
in direct speech? For example, the first sentence would be: 'I feel
hungry,' said Jez.

1. Jez said he felt hungry.

2. Mrs Trott told us to sit down.

3. Dad told me not to eat any more cake.

4. Fergus said his brother was ill.

5. Freya said she couldn't come with us.

Matching subjects and verbs

Most sentences contain a verb (or action word) and a subject (the person or thing doing the action). These two parts of the sentence need to match, or 'agree'.

Subject and verb agreement

When the subject of a sentence is singular, the verb must be singular too. If the subject is plural, it must be matched by a plural verb.

The cactus is prickly.

singular subject — singular verb

The camels are grumpy.

plural subject — plural verb

Sometimes it's hard to work out whether a subject is singular or plural. This can lead to mistakes with subject and verb agreements.

Singular or plural?

When the subject of a sentence is a group of words (a noun phrase), it can be hard to match the subject with the verb. For example, which of these sentences looks right to you?

A line of camels are crossing the desert.

A line of camels is crossing the desert.

The correct sentence is on the right because the noun phrase is singular. (The subject is the line, not the camels.)

You can check whether a noun phrase is singular or plural by turning a statement into a **question**.

singular verb — singular noun phrase

Is a line of camels crossing the desert? ✓

plural verb — singular noun phrase

Are a line of camels crossing the desert? ✗

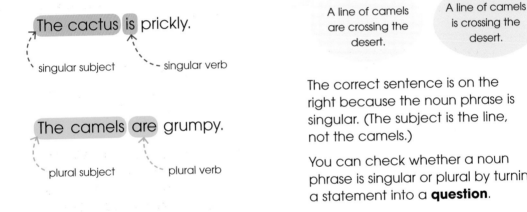

Find out more about: **subjects and verbs** (page 22); **noun phrases** (page 54).

'There was' or 'There were'?

When a sentence begins with the word 'There', the subject comes **after** the verb. This can make it tricky to match the verb with its subject.

Check the words **directly after** the verb to make sure they agree with the verb.

singular verb ⸱⸱⸱ ⸱⸱⸱ plural subject

There was some lizards on the rock. ✖

This sentence is wrong because the verb doesn't match the subject.

plural verb ⸱⸱⸱ ⸱⸱⸱ plural subject

There were some lizards on the rock. ✔

This sentence is correct because the subject and verb agree.

More than one subject?

Some sentences appear to have a plural subject, when in fact their subject is singular. Watch out for **linking words** that can cause confusion.

- When two or more people or things are linked by the word 'and', they form a **plural** subject.

plural verb

Here come the news reporter and her crew.

linking word 'and'   plural subject

- When a person or thing is linked to other people or things by the phrases 'with', 'along with' or 'as well as', it's a **singular** subject. The other people or things are simply added to the subject.

singular verb

Here comes the news reporter with her crew.

linking word 'with'   addition to the subject   singular subject

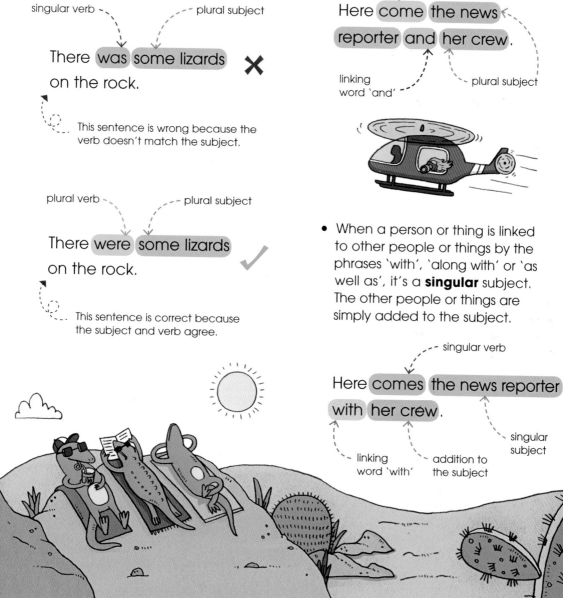

65

Tricky pronouns

When the subject of a sentence is a pronoun like 'everyone', it can be hard to decide whether it's singular or plural. This can lead to mistakes in making subjects and verbs agree.

These pronouns are **singular** and must be matched with a singular verb:

anyone	somebody
everyone	no one
everybody	each

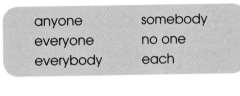

Everyone **is** here.

singular subject — singular verb

These pronouns are **plural** and need a plural verb:

many	both
few	some
several	others

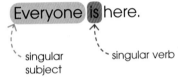

Few of us **are** swimming.

plural subject — plural verb

In the past, the pronoun **none** was always used with a singular verb. Nowadays, however, people often use it with a plural verb.

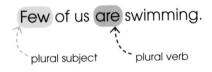

None of my friends is sporty.
None of my friends are sporty.

Both these versions are used.

Some and all

The words 'some' and 'all' can be singular **or** plural, depending on what they refer to.

Ask yourself the question: Can I count the thing 'some' or 'all' refers to? If it **can** be counted, the verb must be **plural**. If it **can't** be counted, the verb is **singular.**

Some of the jigsaw pieces **are** lost.

plural subject (the pieces can be counted) — plural verb

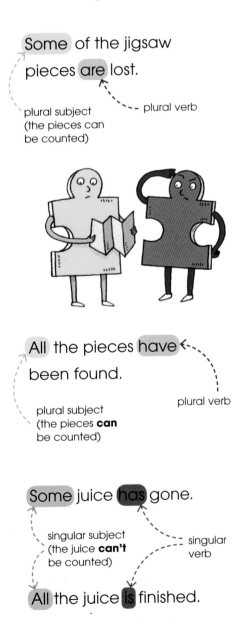

All the pieces **have** been found.

plural subject (the pieces **can** be counted)

plural verb

Some juice **has** gone.

singular subject (the juice **can't** be counted) — singular verb

All the juice **is** finished.

Test yourself on matching subjects and verbs

How well can you match subjects and verbs? Use a pen and paper for these quizzes, then check your answers on page 132.

 1 Making subjects and verbs agree

Look at the sentences below, then write them out for yourself. Can you make the verbs match the subjects?

1. Some of my friends want / wants to go to the beach.

2. Is / Are Izzy and her sister coming too?

3. There was / were seven chocolates left in the box.

4. Only a few of us know / knows how to get there.

5. A sack of potatoes was / were left in the shed.

2 Right or wrong?

All eight verbs in this passage are in bold type, but only four of them match their subject. Can you spot the **four** verbs that **don't** match their subject?

The captain and his team really **want** to win. Several players **are** good at passing. A few **are** good at shooting goals, but nobody **have** any idea about marking, and someone always **drop** the ball. Everyone, including the supporters, **work** hard, but no matter how hard everybody **tries**, the Barrington Battlers always **comes** bottom of the league.

Get it right

The English language can be tricky to use, but you can avoid some common mistakes if you follow the guidelines here.

'Could have' or 'could of'?

Most people shorten the word 'have' when they're speaking, so 'I could have screamed' becomes 'I could've screamed'. When this shortened version is written down, it's sometimes written as 'could of', but this is a mistake. It's also wrong to write 'should of' and 'would of'.

I **could of** skated for hours. ✗

I **could have** skated for hours. ✓

'Try to' or 'try and'?

When people are speaking, they often use the verb **try** followed by the conjunction 'and'. This is not a problem in speech, but it shouldn't be used in formal written English. Instead, the verb **try** should be followed by the preposition **to**.

I will **try and** come home early. ✗

I will **try to** come home early. ✓

Learn and teach

The verb **learn** is sometimes used incorrectly, as if it meant 'teach'.

- You **can** learn a subject or a skill.

  We **learn** French. ✓

- You **can** teach someone a subject or a skill.

  Miss Poodle **teaches** us French. ✓

- You **can't** 'learn' someone a subject or a skill.

  Miss Poodle **learns** us French. ✗

Bring and take

If a person, an animal or an object is being moved **towards** something, you use the word **bring**.

> Don't forget to bring your kite to my house.

If someone or something is being moved **away**, you use **take**.

> We can take our kites to the park.

Lay and lie

The verb **lie** means to place **yourself** in a horizontal position. Its past simple form is 'lay'.

> Casey went to **lie** down.
> She **lay** on her bed.

The verb **lay** means to place **someone or something** in a horizontal position. Its past simple form is 'laid'.

> Mum went to **lay** the baby in his cot. She **laid** him on his back.

It is **not** correct to say:

> Casey went to **lay** down. ✗

Sat and stood

The words **sat** and **stood** are the past simple forms of the verbs 'sit' and 'stand'. This means they can be used on their own, but they **can't** be used with 'am', 'are', 'was' or 'were'.

> I **sat** on the sofa. He **stood** on the rug. ✓

> I am **sat** on the sofa. He was **stood** on the rug. ✗

When you are using 'am', 'are', 'was' or 'were', you need to use the verb forms 'sitting' and 'standing'.

> I am **sitting** on the sofa. He was **standing** on the rug. ✓

Using 'done'

People sometimes have problems using the word **done**.

Instead of saying:

> He **did** a good job. ✓
> ⌃
> `- - - past simple`

Or:

> He has **done** a good job. ✓
> ⌃
> `- - - past participle`

They say:

> He **done** a good job. ✗
> ⌃
> `- - - past participle`

Because **done** is a past participle, it **can't** be used **on its own**. It can only be used with 'have', 'has' or 'had'.

Find out about: **past simple** (page 24); **past participles** (page 26).

Using 'them'

The word **them** is a **pronoun** that takes the place of a plural noun.

For example, in the sentence 'Give me the socks', you can replace 'the socks' with the pronoun 'them'.

However, it's **not** correct to replace the word 'the' (the definite article) with the word 'them':

Instead, you need to say:

Using 'myself'

The word **myself** is a **reflexive pronoun** that's used with the subject 'I'.

It can be used:

- to reflect back on its subject

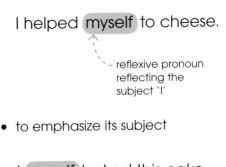

reflexive pronoun reflecting the subject 'I'

- to emphasize its subject

I **myself** baked this cake.

reflexive pronoun strengthening the subject 'I'

However, the word 'myself' **can't** be used when the subject of the sentence isn't 'I'.

Mum made tea for Ben and **myself**.

It's also a mistake to use 'myself' as the subject of a sentence.

Myself and the team worked hard.

Instead, you should say:

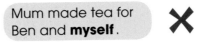

Mum made tea for Ben and **me**.

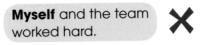

The team and **I** worked hard.

In and into

As a general rule, you use the word **in** when a person or thing is **already** in a place.

> Nina is in the garden. She has a mouse in her pocket.

You use the word **into** to show that a person or thing is **moving** from one place into another.

> Hari stuffed his towel into the locker and jumped into the pool.

The words **on** and **onto** follow the same rules as 'in' and 'into'.

> Jade is sitting on her horse.
> Gemma is climbing onto hers.

Double negatives

Negatives are words like 'no', 'not' or 'nobody'. They are very useful, but if they're used wrongly they can change the meaning of a sentence.

- If you use a **single** negative in a sentence, it gives the sentence a **negative meaning**.

I am eating.   I am **not** eating.

positive   negative

- If you use **two negatives** in the same sentence, they **cancel** each other out, so the sentence loses its negative meaning.

first negative

I'm **not** eating **nothing**. ✗

second negative

This sentence means 'I'm eating something'.

To make these sentences negative, you need to **replace** the second negative with a different word:

I can't see no ghosts.	✗	I can't see any ghosts.	✓
No one did nothing.	✗	No one did anything.	✓
We didn't go nowhere.	✗	We didn't go anywhere.	✓

Don't confuse...

Some words are easy to confuse because they sound the same. Watch out for these common confusing words.

It's/its

- **it's** is the **shortened** form of 'it is' or 'it has'. It has an **apostrophe** to show where a letter or letters are missed out.

- **its** is a **possessive**, meaning 'belonging to it'.

shortened form of 'it has'

It's been racing round the rocks and now it's chasing its tail!

shortened form of 'it is'

possessive

They're/their/there

- **they're** is the **shortened** form of 'they are'. It has an **apostrophe** showing a missing letter.

- **their** is a **possessive**, meaning 'belonging to them'.

- **there** is an **adverb of place** that describes where something is. It is also used to **introduce** someone or something, as in the phrase 'There he is!'

adverbs of place

There are two baby dinosaurs over there. I think they're laughing at their father.

possessive

shortened form of 'they are'

Find out more about: **apostrophes** (pages 90); **possessives** (page 91); **adverbs** (page 36).

You're/your

- **you're** is the **shortened** form of 'you are'.

- **your** is a **possessive**, meaning 'belonging to you'.

You're in charge of your team.

shortened form of 'you are'

possessive

Who's/whose

- **who's** is the **shortened** form of 'who is' or 'who has'.

shortened form of 'who is'

Who's sleeping in my bed?

Who's been eating my cake?

shortened form of 'who has'

- **whose** can have two different roles in a sentence.

  It can be a **possessive**, meaning 'belonging to who'.

  Whose dog is it?

  It can also be a **relative pronoun**, standing for a person that something belongs to.

  This is the boy whose jeans are so baggy.

Passed/past

It's easy to confuse the words **passed** and **past** because they sound the same, even though they have different spellings.

- **passed** is always used as a **verb**.

verb

Mrs Gumdrop passed me a note saying I had passed the test.

verb

- **past** can be used in four different ways. It can be:

a **noun**

In the past, people didn't wash very often.

an **adjective**

I've watched four matches in the past week.

a **preposition**

The children tiptoed past the sleeping giant.

an **adverb**

Everyone cheered as the princess drove past.

Find out more about: **relative pronouns** (page 16).

All ready/already

People can have problems choosing between **all ready** and **already**.

- **all ready** is a **phrase** meaning 'completely prepared'.

  I've found my coat and I'm all ready to go.

- **already** is an **adverb of time**, showing that something has happened before a certain time.

  It's time to go. I've already got my coat.

All together/altogether

The words **all together** and **altogether** can sometimes cause confusion.

- **all together** is a **phrase** meaning 'everybody doing something at the same time'.

  Let's sing this all together.

- **altogether** is an **adverb of degree**, meaning 'completely'.

  I feel altogether confused.

Lose/loose

The words **lose** and **loose** sound similar, but they have completely different meanings.

I don't want to lose my phone.

'lose' is a verb.

This dress is much too loose.

'loose' is usually an adjective.

Homonyms – words that sound the same

Words that sound the same but have different meanings are called **homonyms**.

- Many homonyms have different spellings, even though they sound exactly the same.

  deer / dear

  knew / new

  waist / waste

  pear / pair

a chilly chilli

- Some homonyms sound the same **and** have the same spelling, but their meanings are very different. Can you think of two different meanings for each of these words?

  bat   nail   seal

Test yourself on tricky and confusing words

You'll need a pen and paper for these tests. When you're happy with your answers, turn to page 132 to check them.

 Fill in the gaps

Can you choose the right word to fill in the gaps in the sentences below?

1. Carly waved at Kez and myself / me .

2. Kenny was the star of the match. He done / did really well.

3. Karen was sat / sitting in the middle of the sofa.

4. I should of / have tried harder to beat the record.

5. The rabbit twitched its / it's nose.

6. Bruno ate a large stake / steak .

 Spot the mistakes

Bob the bicycle repair man has left a note, but he's so upset he's made **twelve** mistakes. Can you find them all?

> Who's bicycle is this? Its covered with rust, the chain has come lose, and you need to change them tyres. If your not careful you'll have an accident. Their are lots of dangers out they're and you might even run in to a tree! Don't go out again until its past it's safety test. I don't want to hear no excuses!

Punctuation

Punctuation marks are signs like full stops, commas, and apostrophes. They divide words into groups and act like signposts, making writing easier to follow.

Making sense

Writing needs punctuation in order to make sense. Try comparing these two versions of the same passage:

This version has **no** punctuation.

whats up said Ed braking hard have you seen that monkey Kate asked its very naughty Ed looked around there were monkeys everywhere where did they come from he asked I have no idea said Kate

This version has been punctuated.

'What's up?' said Ed, braking hard.
'Have you seen that monkey?' Kate asked.
'It's very naughty.'
Ed looked around.
There were monkeys everywhere.
'Where did they come from?' he asked.
'I have no idea!' said Kate.

Punctuation marks

These are the main punctuation marks used in written English:

.
full stop

!
exclamation mark

?
question mark

,
comma

:
colon

;
semicolon

' '
quotation marks

'
apostrophe

( )
brackets

—
dash

-
hyphen

...
ellipsis

These are some other useful punctuation marks:

- **& / @ * #**

Capital letters and **lower case letters** also play an important role in punctuation. (Capitals are also known as upper case letters.)

Places to pause

Some punctuation marks show you where to pause in your reading. They point out the places where you might take a breath if you were reading aloud.

commas show a short pause

Hugo ate a banana,
a pear and a large,
crunchy green apple.
Then he fell asleep.

full stops mark a longer break

Points of view

Punctuation marks can give helpful clues about the writer's point of view.

Look at the way these three punctuation marks change the meaning of a simple sentence:

It's finished.

A full stop shows that this is a statement.

It's finished?

A question mark indicates a question.

It's finished!

An exclamation mark expresses surprise or delight.

Full stops

Full stops go at the end of a sentence to show that it is finished. They mark the place where you would probably take a breath if you were reading aloud.

Using full stops

Full stops mark the end of a complete statement. All sentences end in a full stop unless they're a question, an exclamation, an interjection or a command.

Something's gone wrong.
statement

I give up!
exclamation

What's this?
question

The instructions were hard to understand.

statement ending in a full stop

Full stops in sentences

Full stops go **directly** after the final word in a sentence. The full stop is followed by a single space and the next sentence starts with a **capital letter**.

We heard a rumble of thunder. It began to rain.

capital letter

full stop followed by a single space

No full stop needed

Notices, labels and lists **don't** have full stops.

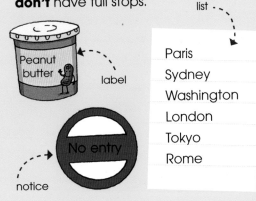

Peanut butter
label

No entry
notice

list

Paris
Sydney
Washington
London
Tokyo
Rome

Shortened words

Some people put a full stop after a word that's been shortened. For example, 'February' can be shortened to 'Feb.' You can learn more about shortened words on page 115.

Different names

Full stops are sometimes called **full points** or **periods**. When a full stop is used in an internet address, it's known as a **dot**.

 Find out more about: **questions** (pages 80-81); **exclamations, interjections and commands** (page 79).

Exclamation marks

Exclamation marks go at the end of an exclamation, an interjection or a command. They are also used to add emphasis to a sentence.

Exclamations

Exclamations **always** end with an exclamation mark. They are sentences expressing a strong emotion, such as surprise, joy, anger, pain or fear.

I'm in trouble!

I win!

You cheated!

Interjections

Interjections like 'Hey!' or 'Ouch!' are followed by an exclamation mark. They are usually just **one word** long.

Commands

Exclamation marks are used in commands when the command is an urgent **order**, rather than a polite instruction.

- Sit up straight!
- Watch out!

Adding emphasis

Some writers use an exclamation mark to show that a sentence is important or surprising.

When they opened the treasure chest, it was completely empty !

Use with care

If you use too many exclamation marks, they will quickly lose their effect. It's often better to use a full stop instead.

The party was fantastic ! I wish you'd been there ! We had so much fun !

There are too many exclamation marks here.

One's enough!

Writers of comics create exciting effects by using lots of exclamation marks in a row, but this kind of punctuation doesn't work in everyday writing.

Find out more about: **interjections** (page 7).

Question marks

Question marks go at the end of a sentence that asks a question. They show the place where you would probably lift your voice a little if you were reading aloud.

Using question marks

The question mark usually goes directly after the last word in a sentence. Then the next word starts with a capital letter.

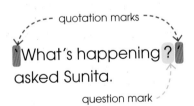

What did Kieran do next? We have no idea.

— capital letter

question mark followed by a single space

Direct and reported speech

Question marks are found in **direct speech** where a question is put inside quotation marks.

quotation marks

"What's happening?" asked Sunita.

question mark

When a question is turned into **reported speech**, you don't use quotation marks and there is **no** question mark.

Sunita asked what was happening.

Spotting questions

There are several different types of question, and they all end with a question mark.

- A question can start with a **question word**, such as how, what, why, where, when, which or who.

Where is Joe?

question word   question mark

- You can create a question by **changing the word order** in a statement so the verb comes first.

Is Joe outside?

verb comes first   question mark

- You can form a question by putting the verb **do** in front of a statement.

Do donkeys like apples?

verb 'do' introduces the question   question mark

Question tags

Question tags are very short questions added to the **end** of a statement. They are separated from the statement by a **comma**, and they end with a question mark.

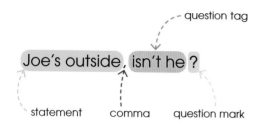

Joe's outside, isn't he ?

question tag

statement   comma   question mark

Question tags often contain shortenings, like 'isn't', 'can't' or 'doesn't'. They are **not** usually found in formal English.

Rhetorical questions

People sometimes ask a question to stress a point, without expecting an answer. This kind of question is called a rhetorical question and it still needs a question mark.

Will he ever remember to shut the door?

Why do I bother?

Could she look any lovelier?

Statement or question?

You can turn a statement into a question simply by putting a question mark at the end of the sentence. This has the same effect as lifting your voice to show that you're asking a question.

statement

The castle is haunted.

The castle is haunted?

question

Showing uncertainty

Some writers use a question mark to show that they're uncertain about a fact, such as a date of birth. The question mark usually goes inside a pair of brackets.

Ivan Edake
Born 1822 (?)
Died 1910

Commas

Commas separate a word or a group of words from the rest of the sentence. They show the place where you would pause very slightly if you were reading aloud.

Making things clear

Commas can play an important role in making meaning clear.

Hailey loves cooking her family and her pets.

This sentence suggests that Hailey loves to cook her family.

Hailey loves cooking, her family and her pets.

This comma makes the real meaning clear.

Commas in lists

Commas are used to separate **single words** in a list. Each word is divided from the next by a comma, except for the last two words, which are linked by the word 'and'.

We need paper, scissors, pens, glue and string.

'and' links the last two words.

Each item is followed by a comma.

Commas are also used to separate **groups of words** in a list.

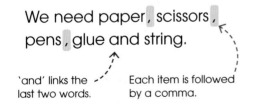

Sid scared the cat, chased the dog, tickled the gerbil and annoyed the hamster.

Commas with 'and'

Usually, the last two items in a list are linked by the word 'and' without a comma in front of it. However, there are some sentences that need an **extra comma** to make their meaning clear.

In the sentence below, the comma shows that Marcia didn't order ice cream flavoured with curry and chocolate!

Marcia ordered soup, chips, curry, and chocolate ice cream.

comma needed here

Commas with conjunctions

A comma is often used in front of a **conjunction** that joins two statements.

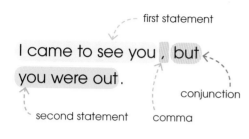

first statement

I came to see you , but

you were out .

conjunction

second statement   comma

These conjunctions often have a comma in front of them:

but	or	while
yet	nor	so

Watch out!

- It's **not** correct to link two statements by a comma **unless** you use a conjunction as well.

Sam wants to be a chef, he tries out lots of recipes.

Sam wants to be a chef , so he tries out lots of recipes.

comma plus conjunction

- You can't use a comma without a conjunction to link two statements, but you can use a conjunction **without a comma** to join short statements that are closely related.

We sat on the bench and ate our picnic.

conjunction with **no** comma

Commas and introductions

Some sentences start with a word or a group of words that sets the scene for the main action. In these sentences, you need a comma **after the introduction** to mark a pause before the action begins.

comma marks a pause

Last week , Oscar baked an amazing cake.

introduction   main action

The comma can follow a single word, a phrase or a clause.

Surprisingly, the cake contained beetroot.

introductory word and comma

After a short pause, we began to eat.

introductory phrase and comma

Once we had tasted it, we wanted more!

introductory clause and comma

Find out more about: **conjunctions** (pages 42-43).

Isolating commas

Sometimes a sentence is **interrupted** by a clause or phrase giving extra information. This information needs a comma on either side of it to show that it's **not essential** to the meaning of the sentence.

The wizard, who was old and cross, stamped his foot.

clause isolated by two commas

Isolating commas always work **in pairs**. They act like brackets, separating the extra information from the rest of the sentence.

first comma

We realized, after a long search, that the key was lost.

second comma   *phrase*

Comma check

It's easy to check that you've used isolating commas correctly. First **remove** the information inside the commas, then see if your sentence still makes sense.

This is what happens to the two sentences above:

The wizard stamped his foot.

We realized that the key was lost.

Both sentences still make sense, so the commas were used correctly.

Watch out!

Some clauses starting with 'who' or 'that' **don't** have isolating commas because they provide information that's **essential** to the meaning of the sentence.

When you remove the clauses from the sentences below, the meaning of the sentences changes:

All the children who had tickets went to the show.

*essential clause with **no** isolating commas*

We only stock fruit that is fresh and ripe in our shops.

Commas and names

If you use someone's name when you're talking directly to him or her, you need to put a comma in front of the name.

Are you coming, Charlie?

comma before the name

If you forget this comma, the meaning of a sentence may change completely.

Let's eat, Granny!

Let's eat Granny!

Test yourself on commas and other punctuation marks

Do you feel confident about punctuation? Use a pen and paper for these quizzes, then turn to page 133 to see the answers.

1 Adding punctuation

This passage needs more punctuation. Can you add **six** full stops, **five** commas, **one** question mark and **one** exclamation mark? You will also need to turn **three** words starting with a lower case letter into words beginning with a capital letter.

> The first time I met Oswin we were on a hiking holiday we had just climbed a long steep and winding path my legs ached my feet hurt and my head throbbed painfully Oswin on the other hand looked as fresh as a daisy 'what's the matter with you' he asked 'I can't go on' I replied

2 Commas needed!

All the commas have been left out of these sentences. Can you work out where they should go? There should be a total of **seven** commas.

> Jemima my oldest friend loves bags watches and bangles. Her hair is thick bright red and wavy. In the summer she dances barefoot in the park. People often stare at her but she doesn't care. In my opinion she's the coolest girl in the school.

Quotation marks

When you write down someone's words, you use quotation marks to show where the words begin and end. Speech inside quotation marks is called direct speech.

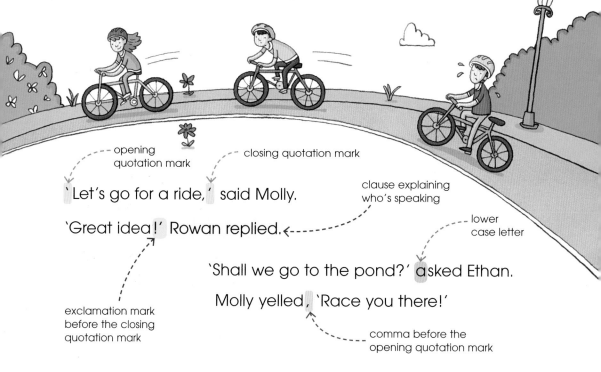

opening quotation mark

closing quotation mark

'Let's go for a ride,' said Molly.

clause explaining who's speaking

'Great idea!' Rowan replied.

lower case letter

'Shall we go to the pond?' asked Ethan.

Molly yelled, 'Race you there!'

exclamation mark before the closing quotation mark

comma before the opening quotation mark

Showing speech

- To show **direct speech**, you put a person's words **inside** quotation marks.

- Each **new** person's speech begins with a **capital letter**.

- Each time somebody new speaks, you need to start a **new line**.

- A speech can end with a comma, an exclamation mark, a question mark or a full stop.

- The punctuation mark at the end of a speech always goes **inside** the closing quotation mark.

Who's speaking?

- Direct speech usually has a **clause**, such as 'Molly said', that explains who's speaking.

- This clause can go before **or** after the speech.

- When the clause goes **after** the speech, it starts with a lower case letter unless it's a person's name.

- When the clause goes **in front** of the speech, it's followed by a comma and a space before the opening quotation mark.

Interrupted speech

Sometimes a clause like 'she said' interrupts a speech. When this happens, the second part of the speech **doesn't** always start with a capital letter.

comma after clause explaining who's speaking

'It seems to me,' said Molly, 'that we're lost.'

no capital letter at the start of the interrupted speech

In some cases, a clause like 'she said' comes between two sentences of speech. Then the second sentence begins with a capital letter.

'Don't worry,' Rowan said calmly. 'Somebody will rescue us before it gets dark.'

This is a new sentence so it starts with a capital letter.

Different names

Quotation marks are also known as **inverted commas, speech marks** or **quotes**.

Breaking up speech

It's a good idea to break up long speeches to make them easier to read. Look at the way this speech is interrupted by clauses and sentences:

clause interrupting speech

sentence interrupting speech

'Don't you realize,' Orlando spluttered wildly, 'the aliens could invade at any time?' He seized me roughly by the shoulders. 'Do you have any idea what that could mean?' I stared back at him blankly. 'It means,' he continued in a doom-laden voice, 'the end of civilization as we know it!'

87

Special words

Quotation marks are useful for highlighting words that are special in some way. They can be used for:

- unusual words or phrases

We call ourselves the 'terrible twosome'.

- foreign words or phrases

We ate 'saucisson' in France.

- words that are meant to be sarcastic or humorous

Our 'luxury' hotel turned out to be a wooden shed.

Titles and names

If you're writing about a book or a film, you can either put its title in quotation marks or you can underline it. (In typed and printed texts, titles and names are usually shown in italics.)

We watched 'Star Trek'. ✓

Both these methods of highlighting a title are correct.

We watched <u>Star Trek</u>. ✓

Which titles and names?

Quotation marks are used for:

- titles of books, magazines and newspapers

Connor's favourite book is 'The Hobbit'. ←

The full stop goes **outside** the quotation marks.

- titles of films, plays and TV programmes

Did you see the last episode of 'Where's Harry?' ←--

If the title ends in a question mark, **don't** add a second question mark.

- names of ships, trains and spacecraft

We sailed on the ←-- 'Gloriana'.

The word 'the' isn't inside quotation marks because it's not part of the ship's name.

Quotations

You also use quotation marks when you're quoting from a piece of writing.

comma before the quote

Shakespeare wrote, 'The course of true love never did run smooth.'

full stop before the closing quotation mark

Colons and semicolons

Colons and semicolons both mark a short pause. It's possible to write without using them at all, but they can be useful.

Using colons

- Colons are often used to **introduce a list**.

You will need: colon introduces the list

eggs

butter   colon marks a pause before the list begins

flour

Make sure you bring: towels, swimming costumes and goggles.

- You can also use a colon to **link two sentences**, when the second sentence helps to explain the first or repeats it in a different way.

We soon solved the mystery of the missing sausages : the dog had eaten them.

second statement explains the first

colon creates a link

- Some writers use a colon to **introduce direct speech**, especially if the speech is very long. However, it's more usual to use a comma.

colon introduces the speech

Kevin said : 'I don't want to see you again.'

Using semicolons

- Semicolons can be used to **separate items in a list** with complicated parts.

At the zoo we saw a huge, hairy gorilla ; an alligator that liked to swim in small circles ; and a very inquisitive, shocking-pink flamingo.

- You can also use a semicolon to **link two sentences** that are close in meaning and have equal importance.

semicolon creates a link

The alligator snapped its jaws ; it was feeding time at the zoo .

two statements with equal importance

Find out more about: **lists** (page 82); **direct speech** (page 58).

Apostrophes

Apostrophes have two different roles. They are used in shortened words (contractions) to show that letters have been left out. They are also used in possessives, to show who or what something belongs to.

Missing letters

A word with an apostrophe to show missing letters is called a **contraction**. Most contractions are shortened forms of a subject plus a verb, such as 'he's' for 'he is'. Contractions are common in everyday speech, but some people avoid them in formal writing.

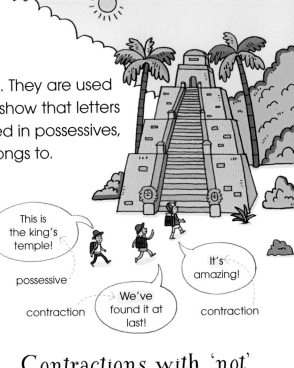

This is the king's temple!

possessive

contraction

We've found it at last!

It's amazing!

contraction

Common contractions

The verbs **be** and **have** are often used as contractions.

I am	I'm
you are	you're
he / she / it is	he's / she's / it's
we are	we're
they are	they're

I have	I've
you have	you've
he / she has	he's / she's
we have	we've
they have	they've

Contractions with 'not'

Some contractions are short forms of verbs used with **not**.

does not	doesn't
cannot	can't
should not	shouldn't

Tricky contractions

These tricky contractions are missing several letters:

I will not	I won't
I would	I'd
I had	I'd

Other uses

Apostrophes are also used for times, such as 'six o'clock', and for some surnames, like O'Connor.

Possessives

When you put an apostrophe after someone's name it shows that something belongs to him or her. This kind of apostrophe is called a **possessive**. You can use a possessive to show that something belongs to a person, an animal or a thing.

To form a possessive for a singular noun, you usually add an **apostrophe** followed by the letter **s**.

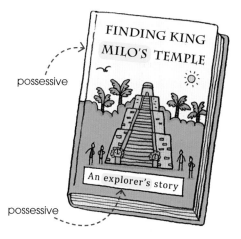

possessive

possessive

No apostrophe needed

Possessives like 'hers' and 'its' already show possession, so they **don't** need an apostrophe.

its	*hers*	*yours*
his	*ours*	*theirs*

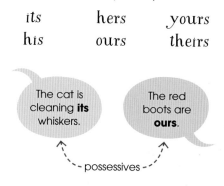

The cat is cleaning **its** whiskers.

The red boots are **ours**.

possessives

Forming possessives

- If the noun is **singular**, add an apostrophe **plus** the letter **s**.

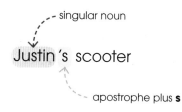

singular noun

Justin **'s** scooter

apostrophe plus **s**

Even if the noun ends in the letter **s**, you still add an apostrophe **plus s**:

The bus **'s** wheels

apostrophe plus **s**

- If the noun is **plural** and ends in the letter **s**, add an apostrophe **after** the **s**:

The girls **'** skates
The babies **'** toys

plural noun ending in **s**

apostrophe after the **s**

- If the noun is **plural** and **doesn't** end in an **s**, add an apostrophe **plus s**:

The mice **'s** whiskers.
The children **'s** boots.

plural noun without an **s**

apostrophe plus **s**

Find out about: **names ending in 's'** (page 92).

Names ending in 's'

For names like James and Marcus that end in a letter **s**, there are two ways to show the possessive.

Either add an apostrophe **plus** an **s**:

> Marcus's fancy dress costume is amazing!

Or add an apostrophe at the **end** of the noun:

> Marcus' fancy dress costume is amazing!

Either way is correct, but you'll need to choose one way and stick to it.

Possessive OR contraction

When you add an apostrophe **plus s** to a person or thing, it can **either** show possession **or** it can be a contraction of the word 'is'.

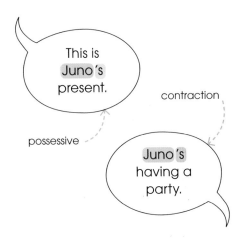

This is Juno's present.

possessive

contraction

Juno's having a party.

Plural or apostrophe?

Some people get confused between plurals and apostrophes. When they add the letter **s** to make a word plural, they sometimes add an apostrophe as well.

Only one of these signs is correct. Can you tell which one it is?

Oranges, apples and bananas

Oranges', apples' and bananas'

Orange's, apple's and banana's

The sign on the left is correct, because the oranges, apples and bananas **don't** need a possessive. (Nothing belongs to them.) So they should simply be plural with an added letter **s** and **no** apostrophe.

Apostrophe test

A good way to decide if a noun needs an apostrophe is to ask the question: Does something belong to it? If the answer is yes, you need an apostrophe.

For example, for the phrase 'Bens boots', first ask the question: Do the boots belong to Ben? As the answer is yes, it's correct to use an apostrophe and write 'Ben's boots'.

Test yourself on quotation marks and apostrophes

Try out these quizzes with a pen and paper. Then check your answers on page 133.

1 Making conversation

Can you use quotation marks to turn this confusing text into a conversation? Remember to start a new line whenever a new person begins talking.

I've got a surprise for you, Kit said. Can you guess what it is? No, I can't, I replied sleepily. I'm sure you'll like it, he said. Open your eyes, he continued, and see what it is. I opened my eyes and gasped. I don't want a parrot! I yelled.

2 Adding apostrophes

Can you write these sentences correctly, using a total of **eight** apostrophes?

1. Hes got his dads nose, hasnt he?

2. Todays the princesss birthday.

3. The dogs licking its paws.

4. Mo wont go to the childrens swimming classes.

3 Find the right word

There are three words to choose from in each of these sentences. Do you think you can pick the right one?

1. This teams / teams' / team's colours are yellow and blue.

2. The men's / mens / mens' hats are unusual.

3. The players / player's / players' aim was to win all their matches.

4. There are three ships' / ship's / ships in the distance.

Brackets and dashes

Writers sometimes use brackets and dashes to add extra information to their sentences. Brackets are always used in pairs, but you can use a single dash or a pair of dashes.

Using brackets

- Brackets can enclose a word, a phrase, a clause or a sentence. They can go in the **middle** or at the **end** of a sentence.

- The words inside a pair of brackets can be an **interruption**, an **explanation** or an **afterthought**.

interruption

explanation

afterthought

We stayed with Keely (who sends her love), and had a balloon ride over Canberra (the capital of Australia) with Tim and Tia. (I think you've met them?)

Extra information

Because the words in brackets give extra information, they can be removed without changing the meaning of the sentence.

Here is the sentence used above, with all the words in brackets taken out:

We stayed with Keely, and had a balloon ride over Canberra with Tim and Tia.

Parentheses

Brackets are sometimes known as parentheses and the information inside them is referred to as **in parenthesis**. The phrase 'in parenthesis' is also used to describe extra information enclosed by dashes or commas.

Watch out!

Sentences with lots of brackets are very hard to read. Try to use them sparingly and never put brackets inside other brackets.

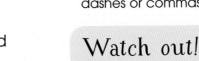

Brackets and full stops

When you're using brackets, it can be hard to decide where to put the full stop.

- If the words in brackets come at the end of a sentence, but don't make a sentence on their own, the full stop should go **after** the closing bracket.

Please bring a snack (bread, cheese and fruit).

full stop **outside** bracket

- If the words in brackets make a complete sentence, put a full stop **inside** the closing bracket. The sentence before the opening bracket must also end with a full stop.

full stop needed here ----

We plan to walk all day. (It will be tiring but fun.) Then we'll camp overnight.

full stop **inside** bracket

new sentence starts after a space

Using dashes

Dashes can be used as a **pair** to separate a word or a group of words from the rest of the sentence.

You use a pair of dashes to enclose words that come in the **middle** of a sentence.

Mario brought some friends – three boys and a girl – on the hike.

dashes separate the extra information from the rest of the sentence

It was – according to Barnaby – a great day out.

Dashes are used like brackets to add information that's **not essential** to the meaning of the sentence. You can remove everything inside a pair of dashes and the sentence will still make sense.

Brackets, dashes or commas?

Extra information can be enclosed by a pair of brackets, dashes or commas, but how do you decide which to use? These guidelines should help you choose.

- **Brackets** create a strong interruption.
- **Dashes** mark a weaker interruption.
- **Commas** cause the least interruption to a sentence.

Single dashes

There are several ways to use a single dash.

- It can mark off **extra information** at the end of a sentence.

  dash introduces
  extra information

  We brought some tools – a screwdriver, a hammer and a saw.

- It can create an **expectant pause** before a new piece of information.

  Crystal opened the box and there inside was – a rabbit!

  dash creates
  a pause

- It can show a **change of direction** in a sentence:

  Alex said it was a goal – Kali wasn't so sure.

  dash marks a
  change of direction

Watch out!

Dashes are very common in emails and notes, but try not to use them too often in formal writing.

Instead of using a dash to show a change of direction, choose one of these alternatives.

- Either start a new sentence:

  Alex said it was a goal. Kali wasn't so sure.

  new sentence

- Or create a subordinate clause introduced by a conjunction like 'but':

  Alex said it was a goal, but Kali wasn't so sure.

  subordinate clause
  introduced by 'but'

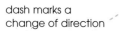

Find out about: **subordinate clauses** (pages 50-51).

Hyphens

Hyphens look like small dashes. They're used for linking two or more words to make a single word or expression. Hyphenated words and expressions can be nouns, adjectives or verbs.

noun

My brother-in-law is test-driving his brand-new truck.

verb

adjective

Hyphenated adjectives

Hyphenated adjectives can only be used **in front** of the noun they describe.

Lisa is a nine-year-old girl.

We explored a tenth-century castle.

When adjectives come **after** a noun, they **can't** be hyphenated, so you need to change the wording of your sentence.

Lisa is nine years old.

We explored a castle that was built in the tenth century.

Well-behaved/ badly behaved

Two-word adjectives starting with 'well' always have a hyphen when they're used in front of a noun. But if you swap 'well' for a word ending in **ly** (such as 'badly'), there is **no** hyphen between the two words.

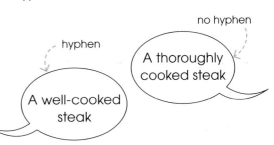

no hyphen

A thoroughly cooked steak

hyphen

A well-cooked steak

Watch out!

Only a very few verbs have a hyphen. Phrasal verbs, like 'give up' or 'take away', are **never** hyphenated.

Hyphens and meaning

In some sentences, you need to use hyphens carefully to make the meaning really clear.

Look at the way the hyphens are used in these two sentences:

There are two year-old horses in that field.

This means there are two horses that are each a year old.

There are two-year-old horses in that field.

This means there are several horses that are each two years old.

Hyphen or no hyphen?

Nowadays, people try to avoid using too many hyphens. This means that many words that once had a hyphen (such as 'ice-cream' and 'e-mail') are now written in a different way. Some hyphenated words have become two separate words (such as 'ice cream'). Some have become single words (such as 'email').

If you're not sure whether a word needs a hyphen or not, look it up in a dictionary.

Avoiding confusion

Some words need a hyphen to avoid confusion.

Watch out!
Man eating dinosaur!

This notice could mean that a man was eating a dinosaur.

Watch out!
Man-eating dinosaur!

This notice makes it clear that the dinosaur eats people.

Different meanings

When two words have the same spelling but a different meaning, using a hyphen can clear up any misunderstanding.

After Granny recovered from her illness, she re-covered the sofa.

hyphen makes the meaning clear

Ellipses and other punctuation marks

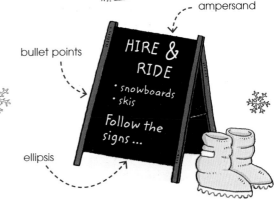

ampersand

bullet points

ellipsis

Ellipsis ...

An ellipsis is formed from three full stops in a row. It shows that a sentence has been left unfinished or that some words have been left out.

You can use an ellipsis to show that a speaker has fallen silent.

> 'I wonder if I could possibly ...'

ellipsis shows the speaker has stopped talking

It can also create a sense of mystery or suspense.

> Stefan opened the door and peered inside ...

ellipsis shows the sentence has deliberately been left unfinished

Writers sometimes use an ellipsis to show that some words are missing. This is especially useful if they're quoting something their readers already know, so they don't need to write it out in full.

> Happy birthday to you ...
> Happy birthday to you!

Ampersand &

The **&** sign stands for the word 'and'. It is sometimes used in shop and company names, but it shouldn't replace 'and' in everyday writing.

RAINBOW & STAR
THE BEST ICE CREAM IN TOWN

Bullet points •

Bullet points are used to introduce items in a list. The items can be single words or short phrases. They don't need to start with a capital letter and they don't need to end with a punctuation mark.

Things to do this week:
* write to Dan
* practise the trumpet
* make a card for Mum
* tidy my room

Forward slash /

You use a forward slash:

- to separate parts of an internet address

- to show alternatives, such as 'boy/girl'

double slash   single slash

http://www.usborne.com/

Please click **yes / no**

forward slash meaning 'or'

'at' sign @

The **@** sign means 'at'. It is used for:

- email addresses
- bills and invoices

INVOICE

Contact: emilygreen@beesure.com

3 hives @ £100 each
1 beekeeper's suit @ £40

Hash sign

The **#** sign represents the word 'number'. It should **never** be used in formal writing.

Sunila is our school's 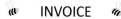#1 sprinter.

This means 'number one'.

Punctuation in social media

Some punctuation marks are used in social media to create an electronic tag. Words with an electronic tag can easily be found in a computer search.

- The # sign goes directly in front of a word or phrase. It's called a 'hashtag' when it's used as an electronic tag.

- The @ sign goes in front of the place or time of a special event.

Join us today! #funrun @49UnionStreetPaxford

@ sign makes the place searchable

hashtag makes the phrase 'funrun' searchable

Asterisk *

The * sign shows that extra information has been provided. The information is usually found in a footnote at the bottom of the page.

asterisk followed by a comma

Look out for kiwis *, parrots and cockatoos.

footnote starts with an asterisk

* Kiwis are rare birds found in New Zealand.

Test yourself on brackets, dashes and hyphens

Are you happy using brackets, dashes and hyphens? Use a pen and paper for these quizzes. The answers are on page 133.

1 Adding brackets

Can you add **a pair of brackets** to each of these statements? Some of them will need a few small punctuation changes too.

1. I played tennis with Max who is nearly fourteen and I won!

2. On the way home, we spotted a snake I think it was an adder.

3. We ate lychees a kind of fruit in China.

4. It took me ages to get home there was a rail strike.

2 Dashes needed

This letter is very hard to read. You can make it much clearer by adding **seven** dashes.

*Ellie has moved to France —
I don't know why. She packed
up all her stuff, books, posters
and clothes before she left.
She didn't tell us she was
going—it was a big surprise.
We waited for a month—which
seemed more like a year
before we heard any news.
Then suddenly, it arrived—
a postcard from Paris!*

3 Missing hyphens

There are **six** hyphens missing from this passage. Can you work out where they should go?

My laid-back brother loves
do-it-yourself projects.
Our house is full of his
badly made, broken-down
furniture. Mum says-he
should smarten up. She's
tired of his couldn't-care-
less attitude.

Writing with style

Grammar and punctuation are essential writing tools, but there are other useful skills that you can learn. The next few pages are filled with suggestions to help you make your writing interesting to read.

Different jobs ~ different styles

Before you start a piece of writing, think hard about the job you want it to do. This will affect the kind of style you use. Here are some examples of different writing styles.

- **novels** tell a story using imaginative language. Novelists describe people, places and actions and show dialogue (conversations). Most novels are divided into chapters.

- **brochures** give information and advice. They are written in clear, simple language and they often have subheadings and lists with bullet points.

- **news reports** provide facts and information. They have a headline that sums up the subject, a brief introduction and very short paragraphs.

- **advertisements** aim to persuade people to buy something or do something. They are written in short, catchy sentences and often include jokes.

Looking at layouts

Some kinds of writing have a special layout that makes them easy to read.

- recipe

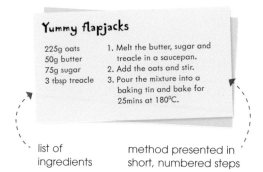

Yummy flapjacks

225g oats	1. Melt the butter, sugar and treacle in a saucepan.
50g butter	2. Add the oats and stir.
75g sugar	3. Pour the mixture into a baking tin and bake for 25mins at 180°C.
3 tbsp treacle	

list of ingredients   method presented in short, numbered steps

- play script

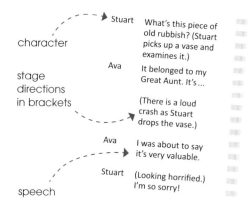

character

| Stuart | What's this piece of old rubbish? (Stuart picks up a vase and examines it.) |

stage directions in brackets

| Ava | It belonged to my Great Aunt. It's... |

(There is a loud crash as Stuart drops the vase.)

| Ava | I was about to say it's very valuable. |

| Stuart | (Looking horrified.) I'm so sorry! |

speech

- letter

address

The Old School
12 Hoot Lane
Doxford
DX1 1AB

20 June 2021   date

Dear Professor Feather
I am writing to say how much I enjoyed your lecture on owls. I had no idea there were so

Different readers

Whenever you start a new piece of writing, ask yourself who will be reading your words. Will it be a child or an adult, a close friend or someone you don't know at all?

Once you know who your audience will be, you can decide on the best way to communicate with them.

Different words

Your choice of words will depend on the job you want your writing to do and the audience you are writing for.

You would use very different kinds of words for:

- a poem about the sea
- a letter applying for a job
- an advertisement for shampoo
- a text to a friend

Hey! Can you buy 3 tix 4 the film? Thx.

No prob!

Let us know when it starts. C u l8r!

Formal or informal?

For some kinds of writing, you need a formal style. For others, a more relaxed, informal style works best. Formal writing follows the rules of grammar and punctuation very strictly. Informal writing is closer to everyday speech – but it should still be free from mistakes!

Informal writing

Informal writing is used in daily life for writing notes or sending messages. People use informal language to communicate with their friends and family.

Hey Jaybee!

How's it going? Check out the pics I took on my trip! They're epic, aren't they?

Cheers,

Jon

- informal writing

Informal writing can include:

- contractions, such as 'How's'
- question tags, like 'aren't they?'
- colloquialisms (words or phrases used in everyday conversation), like 'check out'
- slang, like 'epic'
- nicknames, like 'Jaybee'

Formal writing

Formal writing is used for information books and official documents. It's also used in schools for writing reports and projects. Writers often use formal language to communicate with a general audience or with someone they don't know very well.

Last summer, Jonathan Jones went on a world tour. He took many photographs to document his travels.

formal writing

In a formal piece of writing you need to:

- use proper names (not nicknames)
- avoid contractions, question tags, colloquialisms and slang
- make sure your grammar and punctuation are correct

Mixing styles

Writing doesn't have to be strictly formal or completely informal. For example, if you were writing a letter to your granny, you would use contractions and colloquialisms, but you probably wouldn't use slang.

Dear Granny

How are you? Aren't these photos great? — colloquialism

I'm really looking forward to catching up with you soon.

Love

Jonathan

contraction

Colloquialisms

Colloquialisms are words and phrases that are used in everyday, relaxed conversation.

hang out	bloke
what's up?	kid

Colloquialisms aren't usually found in formal writing, but they are used in stories and plays to make the characters' speech sound more realistic.

Slang

Slang is everyday language that's very informal. It's rarely found in formal written English, except when writers are using dialogue.

Often, people from a specific group, such as teenagers, create their own slang words.

Wicked!

Sweet!

Idioms

Idioms are everyday phrases and sayings. They don't always have an obvious meaning, but they are used so often that they're usually easy to understand. Idioms are often used in informal writing, but it's best to avoid them in formal writing.

Many idioms feature animals. Here are a few examples:

She's got a bee in her bonnet.

Don't be a copycat!

A little bird told me...

Hold your horses!

Choosing words

One way of making your writing come to life is to use a variety of interesting words. Fortunately, the English language has thousands of words to choose from.

Using synonyms

Often, several words share the same meaning. For example, 'surprised', 'amazed' and 'astonished' all mean roughly the same thing. A word with the same meaning as another word is called a synonym. By using a range of synonyms, you can add variety and interest to your writing.

This sentence has three exciting synonyms for 'travelled'.

Zappi raced through the streets, whizzed between towers and zoomed under bridges.

Varying words

If you use the same words over and over again, your writing will soon become monotonous. You can avoid this by using a range of synonyms.

Can you find six synonyms for the word 'ate' in this passage?

Miranda devoured a hearty breakfast. She guzzled her porridge, munched her toast, gobbled her eggs, chomped her bacon, and wolfed down a sausage.

Avoiding overused words

It's a good idea to use a synonym to replace an overused word like 'great'. Here are some common overused words with their synonyms.

great — terrific, wonderful, marvellous, remarkable, outstanding, excellent

happy — cheerful, contented, delighted, thrilled, jubilant, overjoyed

big — large, vast, huge, gigantic, towering, immense, enormous

Choosing the right word

When you have a choice of synonyms, you can pick the best word to suit the style of your writing.

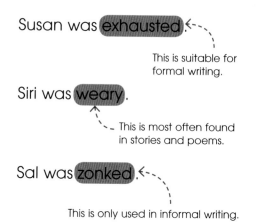

Susan was exhausted.

This is suitable for formal writing.

Siri was weary.

This is most often found in stories and poems.

Sal was zonked.

This is only used in informal writing.

Finding synonyms

If you need a synonym for a particular word, you can look up the word in a **thesaurus**. You'll see a list of synonyms with notes to show when a word is informal or slang.

Watch out!

Before you choose a synonym, make sure it has the right meaning for your sentence. For example, you could use 'kind' and 'friendly' as synonyms for 'nice' in the phrase 'a nice person', but they wouldn't work in the phrase 'a nice meal'!

Hello there!

A friendly meal ✗

Using antonyms

An antonym is a word with the opposite meaning to another word.

Here are some common antonyms:

slow	fast
hot	cold
good	bad
light	dark
happy	sad
rough	smooth
true	false
strong	weak

Using antonyms can add drama and contrast to your writing. Can you spot four pairs of antonyms in the passage below?

Inside the quiet, empty transporter, there was a feeling of calm. Outside, there was chaos in the noisy, crowded streets.

Special effects

On these two pages, you'll find some useful techniques to make your writing more exciting.

pop!

Sound effects

The way a word sounds can have a powerful effect. Try reading this sentence aloud and notice how the sounds bring the description to life:

BANG

fizz

> Patsy produced a potion
> that popped and fizzed
> and gurgled.

The techniques used here are **alliteration**, **onomatopoeia** and **repetition**. They are found in many kinds of writing, but they work especially well in poetry.

Alliteration

Alliteration is the repeating of the same letter sound to create an interesting effect.

> **S**asha **s**at **s**ipping **s**oda
> by the **s**ea.

Onomatopoeia

Onomatopoeia (pronounced 'on-uh-mat-uh-pee-ah') is the use of words to imitate the sound that they describe.

> snap   thump   boom
> ping   quack

Repetition

Repetition is the deliberate repeating of the same words, or very similar words, to create a dramatic effect.

> The rats gnawed and
> nibbled. Then they gnawed
> and nibbled some more until
> the wire was broken.

(Lots of repeated words will make your writing sound boring, but some repetition can be very effective.)

nibble   *nibble*

Making comparisons

Comparisons create a picture with words. Notice how the comparisons in this sentence help you to imagine how Jim looks:

> Jim has a face like a dinner plate, and matchstick legs.

Comparisons can be **similes** or **metaphors**.

Similes

A simile compares two things, using words such as 'like', 'as', 'as though' or 'as if'.

> Greg was as happy as a hippo in a mud bath.

simile introduced by 'as'

simile introduced by 'like'

> Lara has hair like a bird's nest, but she acts as if she's a princess.

simile introduced by 'as if'

Metaphors

A metaphor compares two things, without using words such as 'like' or 'as'. Instead, it describes people or things as if they really were something else.

> Claire is a walking dictionary.

> A golden ball blazed in the sky.

> A blanket of snow covered the hills.

Personification

When you use a phrase like 'the flames danced', you are imagining that something non-human can behave like a person. This technique is called personification. Can you see how it works in this sentence?

> The wind howled, the thunder grumbled and the trees bowed low.

Sentences and paragraphs

When you plan your writing, you need to think carefully about how you divide it into sentences and paragraphs.

Changing pace

Try to vary the length of your sentences. This will make your writing sound lively and interesting.

The twins stumbled into the cave. It was cold and dark and there was a distant sound of dripping water. Zoë shuddered. She felt very frightened and wondered if they would ever get out alive.

Longer sentences are useful for descriptions, thoughts and ideas.

Short sentences are good for showing actions.

New beginnings

If most of your sentences start the same way, your writing will soon become very boring. You can keep your reader interested by using a range of different openings.

Daniel walked for miles. **He** was very tired, but he didn't stop to rest. **He** heard a sudden shout. **He** saw a man in the distance.

Daniel walked for miles. **Even though** he was very tired, he didn't stop to rest. **Suddenly**, he heard a shout. **There** was a man in the distance!

This passage sounds dull because most of its sentences start with 'He'.

This version sounds more dramatic because each sentence starts in a different way.

Long sentence alert!

It's good to mix short sentences with longer ones, but always keep a lookout for very long sentences. If a sentence is hard to read out loud, it's almost certainly too long. Try dividing it into shorter sentences.

Using paragraphs

When you divide a long chunk of writing into paragraphs, it becomes much easier to read.

Paragraphs link a set of sentences that are **related** to each other. It's a good idea to start a new paragraph when:

- a new idea or topic is introduced
- something new happens in a story
- a different character, place or time is introduced

Making links

Writers often use words or phrases to create a link between two sentences or between one paragraph and the next. These linking words are sometimes known as **connectives**.

Here are some useful linking words and phrases:

as a result   meanwhile
however   finally

Signposts for readers

Linking words and phrases usually go at the **start** of a sentence or paragraph. They introduce a new subject, but they also look back to what has gone before.

Archie settled down to sleep. Meanwhile, Lottie was searching frantically for him.

linking word or phrase followed by a comma

The polar ice caps are shrinking. As a result, sea levels are rising.

Different links

Linking words and phrases can be used to:

- put events or ideas **in order**

first	while
next	finally
then	afterwards

- **introduce** a new point or idea

therefore
consequently
as a result

- **contrast** different points of view

however
nevertheless
on the other hand

The writing process

If you want to produce a really good piece of writing, you'll need to work through several different stages. Even professional writers can't get it right first time!

Gathering ideas

The first step in the writing process is to note down all your ideas. You can decide later which ones you want to use.

You may choose to work on your own, or you may prefer working in a group.

Using a mind map

Some people use a **mind map** to organize their ideas.

Write your topic in the middle of a large sheet of paper. Then note down your ideas. Draw lines between the ideas to show how they are connected.

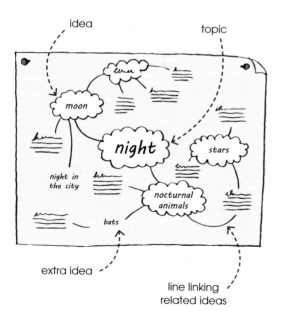

idea

topic

moon

night

stars

night in the city

nocturnal animals

bats

extra idea

line linking related ideas

Making a plan

After you've gathered all your material, you can make a plan. Think about:

- the **introduction** (how your writing will start)
- what you'll put in each **paragraph**
- the **conclusion** (how your writing will end)

Check that the paragraphs are in the right order so they flow naturally.

Writing a draft

Once your plan is ready, you can start working on your first **draft**. This is a rough version of your final text. You may need several drafts before you're happy with your writing.

Strong starts

If you use a punchy opening sentence, you will make your readers keen to find out more.

For example, if you're writing a story, you could plunge straight into the action.

It was the worst moment in Danny's life.

Editing your work

Editing is an essential part of the writing process. It's a chance to spot any mistakes and to make your writing sparkle.

- Read through your draft several times, asking yourself the questions in the checklist below. (You may find it helpful to read your work out loud.)

- If possible, ask someone else to read your work too.

- Note down any problems. Then go back and fix them.

- After you've made all your corrections, read through your work one more time – just to be sure there are no more problems.

Rewriting

When you've completed the editing process, it's time to write out your finished piece of work.

Danny hauled himself out of the seething waves and collapsed, sobbing, onto the rocks. The shark was nowhere to be seen. He was safe at last!

Editing checklist

As you check your work, ask yourself these questions:

 Is my writing easy to follow and understand?

 Are the ideas in the right order?

 Do the links between the paragraphs work?

 Do my sentences make sense? (If you stumble when you read, you'll need to check your grammar.)

 Have I varied the length and structure of my sentences?

 Are there too many overused words? (Think about the best possible words to use.)

 Is my writing grammatically correct? (For example, do the subjects and verbs agree?)

 Have I used punctuation correctly? (Check that your punctuation marks don't create awkward breaks.)

 Are there any spelling mistakes? (Use a dictionary to check tricky spellings.)

Numbers, dates and times

Numbers

Here are some rules to remember when you're using numbers in formal writing.

- Numbers **up to ten** are always written as words.

  I have three brothers.

- Numbers **between ten and ninety-nine** can be shown as numbers **or** figures, but you'll need to stick to one or the other.

  Fatima's sister is 22.

  Mike is twenty-two.

  hyphen needed here

- Numbers **over a hundred** are usually shown in figures.

  There are 365 days in the year.

- If a number comes at the **start** of a sentence, it should always be written as a word.

  Two hundred and twenty-two tickets were sold.

Dates

The usual way to write a date in British English is to start with the day, followed by the month and then the year. In American English, the month goes before the day, and there is a comma before the year.

1 April 2020

British English - no comma here

April 1, 2020

American English - comma before year

Time

To show a **precise** time, use figures followed by **am** for times before midday and **pm** for times after midday.

The train leaves at 11.25 am and arrives at 2.17 pm.

full stop separates hours and minutes

space before pm

If you're showing time in hours, quarters and halves, you can use words **or** figures.

The train leaves at half past seven in the evening.

The train leaves at 7.30 pm.

Shortened words

The English language contains hundreds of shortened words. Sometimes, a word is shortened by having some of its letters removed. Sometimes, two or more words are shown as a set of initials.

abbreviation for 'Saturday'

on Sat. 8 Jan. at 49 Sidney St starting at 4pm

PS Prize for best costume!

initials for 'post script' (Latin for 'extra message')

contraction for 'Street'

Abbreviations and contractions

- **Abbreviations** are words with their endings removed. They generally end in a full stop.

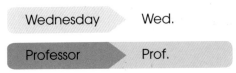

Wednesday → Wed.

Professor → Prof.

- **Contractions** are words with some letters missed out. They are **not** usually followed by a full stop.

Mister

Limited

Saint

Mr Jolly
Glossops Ltd
St Michael's Rd

Road

Latin words

We often use the initials of Latin words in our everyday language. Here are a few examples with their English meanings:

eg   for example
ie   that is
am   morning

Initials and acronyms

Names of countries, organizations and products are often shortened to a set of initials. Usually, the initials all have capital letters without full stops.

We watched two DVDs about the USA.

Digital **V**ersatile **D**isc

United **S**tates of **A**merica

Some words are created by combining the sounds made by initials or by mixing initials with parts of words. These words are known as **acronyms**.

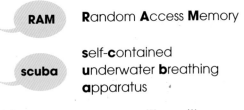

RAM   **R**andom **A**ccess **M**emory

scuba   **s**elf-**c**ontained **u**nderwater **b**reathing **a**pparatus

Many acronyms are written with capital letters. You can check their spelling in a dictionary.

A short guide to spelling

Spelling English words can be tricky, but there are some patterns that are helpful to learn. This guide provides some useful spelling patterns and shows how letters are used to represent different sounds.

Vowels and consonants

The letters of the alphabet can be divided into **vowels** and **consonants**. The five vowels are:

a   e   i   o   u

All the other letters are consonants.

Most words are made from a mixture of consonants and vowels, and almost every English word contains at least one vowel.

Consonant OR vowel

The letter **y** can act as a consonant or a vowel, depending on its position in a word.

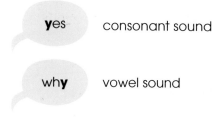

yes   consonant sound

wh**y**   vowel sound

Vowel sounds

Vowel sounds are **not** the same as vowels, although vowels help to spell most vowel sounds. Altogether, there are more than 15 vowel sounds in the English language, and most of them have several different spellings.

Guide to vowel sounds

Here are some common vowel sounds with a range of their spellings:

sound	spellings
ai	wait, cake, day, they
air	chair, care, bear, there
ar	car, father, palm
ee	peel, compete, field
eer	ear, pier, deer, here
igh	pie, kite, bright, mind
oo	too, true, rude, spoon, you
oa	boat, hole, toe, glow, dough
or	fork, saw, your, oar, walk, door, brought, core
ur	turn, her, bird, word, early
yoo	you, few, tube, music

'i' and 'e'

When you use the letters **i** and **e** to make the long sound 'ee', the **i** usually goes **before** the **e**, except when the letters come after the letter **c**.

bel**ie**f p**ie**ce ch**ie**f rece**i**ve ce**i**ling

Sounds made by consonants

Consonants can show a sound:

- with a single letter, like the **b** in bed and tab
- with two letters, like the **sh** in ship and fish
- with three letters in a row, like the **tch** in itch

'c' and 'g'

The letters **c** and **g** don't always make the same sound at the start of a word.

- When they are followed by **e, i** or **y**, they usually make a **soft** sound:

  circus cycle giraffe gem

- When they are followed by any other vowels, they usually make a **hard** sound:

  carrot corn goal gun

Tricky consonant pairs

Some consonant pairs create surprising sounds. Watch out for these tricky combinations.

- **ph** and **gh** can sound like **f**:

  physics, photograph, rough

- **ge** and **dge** can sound like **j**:

  gerbil, page, fudge

- **ch** can sound like **ch, sh** or **k**:

  church, chef, chemist

- **sc** can sound like **sc** or **s**:

  scan, scene, descend

Silent letters

Lots of English words contain letters you can't hear. Here are some common silent letters to watch out for.

silent letter	letter position	example words
b	after m before t	lam**b** de**b**t
g	before n	**g**nat, si**g**n
k	before n	**k**nee
p	before n before s	**p**neumonia **p**sychiatrist
w	before r before h	**w**rong **w**hole

Patterns to remember

- The letter **q** is **always** followed by the letter **u**.

  queen **qu**iet **qu**ilt

- The letters **h, j, k, q, v, w, x** and **y** are **never** doubled in an English word.

Prefixes

A prefix is a group of letters that can be added to the **beginning** of a word to change its meaning.

prefix

re + appear = **re**appear

new word meaning
'appear again'

Here are some prefixes with their meanings:

prefix	meaning	examples
re	again	**re**think, **re**use
over	too much	**over**eat, **over**do
sub	below	**sub**way, **sub**marine
pre	before	**pre**view, **pre**pay

Making opposites

Prefixes are often used to give the **opposite** meaning to a word. These are some common negative prefixes:

prefix	prefix + word
un	**un**well, **un**likely
dis	**dis**honest, **dis**appear
in	**in**correct, **in**visible
mis	**mis**understand, **mis**take

Suffixes

A suffix is a group of letters that can be added to the **end** of a word to change the way it's used. Suffixes can change a word from one word class to another.

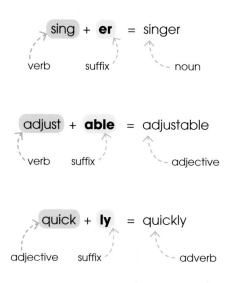

sing + **er** = singer
verb   suffix   noun

adjust + **able** = adjustable
verb   suffix   adjective

quick + **ly** = quickly
adjective   suffix   adverb

Suffix guidelines

- When you add a suffix to a short word ending in a single vowel plus a single consonant, the final consonant is **doubled**.

  run + er = ru**nn**er

  cut + ing = cu**tt**ing

- When you add a suffix to a word ending in the letter **e**, you usually drop the final **e**.

  write + er = writ**er**

  love + able = lov**able**

Final 'y' alert!

Before you add a suffix to a word ending in **y**, you need to think carefully.

- If there's a **consonant** before the letter **y**, change the **y** to **i** and then add the suffix.

  rely + able   =   reliable

- If there's a **vowel** before the **y**, just add the suffix.

  enjoy + able   =   enjoyable

- If the suffix begins with the letter **i**, drop the **y**.

  apology + ize   =   apologize

-tion/-sion/-ssion

Some spellers have problems knowing whether to use the suffix **-tion**, **-sion** or **-ssion**. Here are some guidelines to help you make the right choice.

Words ending in **-t** or **-te** use **-tion**:

collec**t**	collec**tion**
loca**te**	loca**tion**

Words ending in **-d**, **-de** or **-se** use **-sion**:

expan**d**	expan**sion**
deci**de**	deci**sion**
confu**se**	confu**sion**

Words ending in **-ss** or **-mit** use **-ssion**:

posse**ss**	posse**ssion**
ad**mit**	ad**mission**

Syllables and spelling

Words can be broken down into blocks of sound, known as syllables.

- The word 'fan' has just one syllable.

- The word 'fantastic' has three syllables (fan-tas-tic).

Dividing a word into syllables can make it much easier to spell.

Spelling practice

It takes lots of practice to become a confident speller. Try following these four simple steps.

1. Read the word out loud, breaking it up into its separate syllables.

2. Look very carefully at how the word is spelled. (Are there any tricky letter combinations?)

3. Cover up the word and write it down.

4. Check to see if you've got your spelling right. (You may have to do this several times.)

Words to remember

It can be helpful to create a funny sentence, like the one below, to help you remember a tricky spelling.

because

b ig
e lephants
c an
a lways
u nderstand
s mall
e lephants

More about grammar

This final section on grammar gives extra information on sentence structure, verbs and nouns.

Sentence parts

Sentences are made from clauses, and they often contain phrases too.

A **clause** is a group of words built around a verb.

A **phrase** is a group of words that adds extra information to a sentence. Many phrases don't contain a verb.

Clauses

The clause is the basic building block of all sentences. A sentence can have just one clause, or it can have two or more clauses linked by a conjunction.

first clause

conjunction linking to second clause

The magician

waved his wand

and the prince

phrase adding information

turned into a green

and warty frog.

Clause patterns

There are **five** common clause patterns.

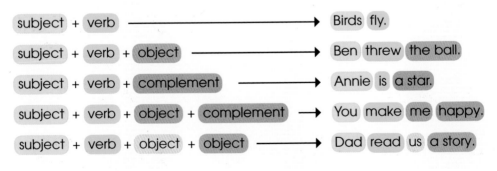

subject + verb ⟶ Birds fly.

subject + verb + object ⟶ Ben threw the ball.

subject + verb + complement ⟶ Annie is a star.

subject + verb + object + complement ⟶ You make me happy.

subject + verb + object + object ⟶ Dad read us a story.

Subject + verb

The simplest pattern for a sentence is a subject plus a verb. The subject goes **before** the verb.

Sylvia screamed.

subject does the action

verb shows the action

Subject + verb + object

Many sentences have a subject, a verb and an object. The object usually follows the verb.

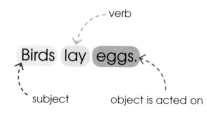

verb

Birds lay eggs.

subject

object is acted on

Subject + verb + complement

A few verbs, like 'be', 'seem' or 'feel', work with a **complement** that tells you more about the **subject**. The complement can be a noun, a noun phrase or an adjective. Verbs that work with complements are known as **linking verbs**.

linking verb

Tim feels sleepy.

subject

complement tells you more about the subject

Subject + verb + object + complement

A small number of sentences have an **object** as well as a **complement**. In these sentences, the complement tells you more about the **object**. (It is sometimes known as the 'object complement'.)

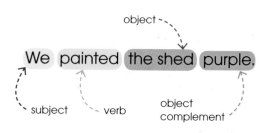

object

We painted the shed purple.

subject

verb

object complement

Subject + verb + object + object

Some clauses have two kinds of object: a direct object and an indirect object.

The **direct object** has the action done to it directly.

The **indirect object** is affected indirectly by the action.

subject

verb

The magician gave Evie a magic compass.

direct object is acted on directly

indirect object is affected indirectly by the action

Find out about: **noun phrases** (page 54).

Phrasal verbs

Phrasal verbs are made by combining a verb with one or more words. You can learn about them on page 33.

Some phrasal verbs are **intransitive** and **don't** have a direct object.

Here are are some examples:

back down	grow up
carry on	keep up
die away	run away
go back	watch out

Many phrasal verbs are **transitive** and have a **direct object**.

- Some **can** be split so the object goes **between** the two parts of the verb. For example, 'I took the book away.'

Some phrasal verbs that **can** be split:

bring up	hand over
cheer up	tell off
cut out	try on
eat up	wear out
give up	write down

- Other phrasal verbs **can't** be split so the object always comes **after** the verb. For example, 'A thief broke into our house.'

Some phrasal verbs that **can't** be split:

come across	go through
face up to	look after
get over	pick on
go over	turn into
hear from	watch out for

Verb inflections

Verbs **inflect** (change their form) to show **person** (I, you, she etc.) and **number** (singular or plural) in the **present tense**.

To form the present tense, add a letter **s** for the **3rd person singular**. Otherwise, the verb stays the same.

singular

1st person	I work
2nd person	you work
3rd person	he/she/it work**s**

plural

1st person	we work
2nd person	you work
3rd person	they work

Verbs change to show the difference between the **present simple** and the **past simple**.

Add **-ed** for the past simple:

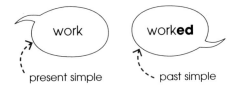

present simple   past simple

Verbs also have inflections for the **present participle** and the **past participle**.

Add **-ing** for the present participle and **-ed** for the past participle:

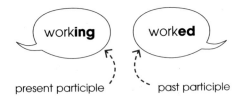

present participle   past participle

Irregular verbs

Not all verbs inflect in a regular way. Here are some irregular verbs with their spellings for the past simple and the past participle.

verb	past simple	past participle
beat	beat	beaten
dig	dug	dug
feed	fed	fed
fight	fought	fought
forget	forgot	forgotten
give	gave	given
hide	hid	hidden
hit	hit	hit
hurt	hurt	hurt
light	lit	lit
ring	rang	rung
shine	shone	shone
tread	trod	trodden

irregular past simple

The bull **trod** lightly through the china shop.

be, have, do

The verbs **be**, **have** and **do** can be the main verb in a sentence, or they can work as an auxiliary (helping) verb. **Auxiliary verbs** work with the main verb to create verb phrases like 'I was working' or 'I do love cheese'.

Tom **had vanished.**

auxiliary verb   main verb

be, **have** and **do** are all **irregular**.

verb forms (present)	be	have	do
1st person sing/plural	am/are	have	do
2nd person sing/plural	are	have	do
3rd person sing/plural	is/are	has/have	does/do

verb forms (past)	be	have	do
1st person sing/plural	was/were	had	did
2nd person sing/plural	were	have	did
3rd person sing/plural	was/were	has/have	did

participles	be	have	do
present participle	being	having	doing
past participle	been	had	done

Words ending in -ing

Words with the ending **-ing** can be:

- the **present participle** of a verb

  Kylie is dancing.

  present participle

- a **verbal noun**, also known as a gerund

  I love dancing.

  verbal noun

Present participles

- The present participle is used to form all the continuous tenses. (See pages 25 to 29.)

- It is also used in a clause without a main verb, known as a **non-finite clause**.

  Gazing out of the window, Kirsty dreamt of home.

  non-finite clause

Verbal nouns

A verbal noun (gerund) can be the subject or the object of a sentence.

Swimming is good for you.

verbal noun as subject

I hate waiting.

verbal noun as object

Unusual and irregular nouns

Most nouns follow the rules for forming plurals explained on page 10. A few nouns, however, have more unusual endings.

- If the noun ends in **-us**, the plural ending is often **-i**.

  cact**us**   cact**i**

- If the noun ends in **-is**, the plural usually ends in **-es**.

  analys**is**   analys**es**

- If the noun ends in **-ix**, the plural nearly always ends in **-ices**.

  append**ix**   append**ices**

- If the noun ends in **-um**, the plural ending is usually **-a**.

  referend**um**   referend**a**

These **irregular nouns** all have major spelling changes:

woman	women
foot	feet
goose	geese
tooth	teeth

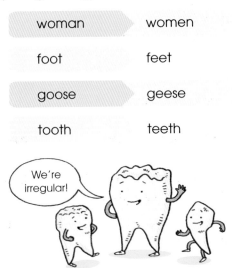

We're irregular!

Glossary

A

abbreviation A word that has been shortened by cutting some letters off the end.

abstract noun A noun that describes something that can't be seen, heard, felt, smelled or tasted.

happiness   hope   talent

acronym A shortened word or phrase made from the initial letters of the original word or phrase.

active voice When a sentence is in the active voice, the subject does the action.

adjective A word that describes a noun or a pronoun.

tall   useful   fierce

adjective phrase Two or more words that give more information about a noun or a pronoun.

adverb A word that affects the meaning of a verb, an adjective or another adverb, answering the questions when, where, how or how often.

slowly   loudly   bravely

adverb phrase Two or more words that include an adverb.

alliteration The repetition of certain letters to create an effect.

ampersand & A symbol that stands for the word 'and'.

antonym A word with the opposite meaning to another word.

apostrophe ' A punctuation mark that shows that one or two letters have been missed out.

article A word that goes in front of a noun and tells you if the noun is specific or general. The three articles are 'a', 'an' and 'the'.

auxiliary verb A 'helping' verb, such as 'be', 'have' or 'do', that combines with a main verb to form a verb phrase.

B

brackets ( ) A pair of punctuation marks used to enclose extra information.

bullet point • A dot before a word, a phrase or a sentence in a list.

C

clause A group of words that contains a subject and a verb. Clauses can be main or subordinate.

collective noun A singular noun that describes a group of people, animals or things.

a **shoal** of fish

colloquialism A word or phrase used in everyday speech and in some informal writing.

colon : A punctuation mark used to introduce a list, to introduce direct speech or a quotation, or to separate two closely linked statements.

comma , A punctuation mark showing a short pause.

command A sentence that gives an order.

common noun A noun used to name a person, thing, place, idea or feeling that is not specific.

comparative The form an adjective or adverb takes when it's used to compare two things or actions.

complement A word or phrase that balances the subject in a sentence, often coming after the verbs 'be' or 'feel'.

complex sentence A sentence made from a main clause plus one or more subordinate clauses.

compound sentence A sentence made from two or more main clauses, joined by a conjunction.

compound word
A word made from two or more other words (for example, 'snowboard').

concrete noun
A noun that names something that can be seen, heard, felt, smelled or tasted.

chair   lemonade   daisy

conjunction A word used to connect words, phrases or clauses.

and   but   however   if

connective A term used to describe conjunctions or phrases that link clauses, sentences and paragraphs.

consonant Any of the letters in the alphabet except the five vowels.

contraction A shortened form of two words, with an apostrophe to show the position of the missing letters.

co-ordinating conjunction A conjunction that joins words, phrases or clauses of equal importance.

D

dash — A punctuation mark showing a break in a sentence. A pair of dashes encloses extra information. A single dash introduces information at the end of a sentence.

definite article The word 'the', used in front of a noun (or a group of nouns) to show that the noun is specific or has already been mentioned.

determiner A word, like 'a', 'the' or 'some', that makes it clear which person, animal or thing is being referred to.

a   the   every   this

direct object A person or thing that is acted on directly by the subject in a sentence.

direct speech In direct speech, you write down the actual words that someone said and usually put the words in quotation marks.

E

ellipsis ... Three dots in a row used to show that some words have been deliberately left out.

exclamation A sentence that expresses a strong feeling, such as surprise, fear, joy or anger.

exclamation mark ! A punctuation mark that goes at the end of an exclamation, and at the end of some commands and interjections.

F

forward slash / A punctuation mark used to show alternatives or to separate parts of an internet address.

full stop . A punctuation mark that goes at the end of a statement.

H

hash sign # A punctuation mark that is used in informal writing to represent the word 'number'.

homonym A word that sounds the same as another word but has a different meaning.

hyphen - A punctuation mark used to link two or more words to make a word or an expression.

a bare bear

I

indefinite article The word 'a' or 'an' used in front of a noun to show that it is not specific.

indefinite pronoun A pronoun that refers to people and things generally, rather than specifically.

indirect object A person or thing that is not acted on directly by the subject in a sentence, but is affected indirectly by the subject's action.

infinitive The basic form of a verb, such as 'go' or 'sing'. The infinitive often has the word 'to' in front of it.

inflection A change in the form of a word.

interjection A word or phrase that stands on its own without a verb and that expresses a strong emotion.

Hey!

intransitive verb A verb that doesn't need an object.

M

main clause A group of words that contains a subject and a verb and makes sense on its own.

main verb The verb that shows the action in a sentence.

metaphor A word or phrase used to describe something as if it were something else.

modal verb A verb, such as 'could' or 'would', that works with a main verb to show something that might happen, rather than something that will definitely happen.

N

negative The opposite of a positive action or statement. 'Not', 'no' and 'none' are all negative words.

noun A word that names a person, an animal, a place, a thing, a feeling or an idea.

noun phrase Two or more words that act in the same way as a noun.

O

object A person, animal or thing that is acted on by the subject in a sentence.

onomatopoeia The use of words that sound like the sound they represent.

quack
quack

P

passive voice When a sentence is in the passive voice, the subject has an action done to it.

past participle The form of a verb that usually ends in '-ed' or '-en'. It is used with the verb 'have' to show actions that happened in the past.

personal pronoun A pronoun, like 'she' or 'it', that stands for a person, an animal, a thing or an idea, without using a name.

personification The transfer of human feelings and characteristics to an object or an idea.

phrasal verb A verb made from a verb plus one or more other words.

keep out   take off   get on

phrase A group of words that adds extra information to a sentence.

plural More than one person or thing (the opposite of singular).

possessive A word showing that something belongs to someone or something.

prefix A group of letters attached to the start of a word that can change its meaning.

preposition A word that shows where something is in relation to something else, or when something happened.

preposition phrase Two or more words that show where something is, when something happened, or how something relates to other things.

present participle The form of a verb that ends in '–ing'. It is used with the verb 'be' to show actions that are continuous.

pronoun A word that stands for a noun or a noun phrase.

proper noun A noun used to name a particular person, place or thing. Proper nouns always start with a capital letter.

Q

question mark ? A punctuation mark that goes at the end of a sentence asking a question.

quotation marks ' ' Punctuation marks that show where a speech begins and ends. They are also used for titles and quotations.

R

relative clause A clause that does a similar job to an adjective, and describes a noun.

reported speech In reported speech, you report what someone said and put it into slightly different words.

S

semicolon ; A punctuation mark that can be used to separate complicated items in a list and to link two statements that are close in meaning.

simile A word or phrase comparing something with something else.

simple sentence A sentence that contains just one verb.

singular A single person or thing (the opposite of plural).

statement A sentence that states a fact or gives a piece of information.

subject The person, animal or thing doing the action in a sentence.

subordinate clause A group of words that contains a subject and a verb and adds meaning to a main clause.

subordinating conjunction A conjunction that introduces a subordinate clause and links it to the main clause.

suffix A group of letters added to the end of a word that can change its meaning.

superlative The form an adjective or adverb takes when it's used to compare more than two things or actions.

fast   faster   fastest

syllable One of the blocks of sound that make up a word.

synonym A word that means the same, or nearly the same, as another word.

T

tense The form a verb takes to show the time when an action happens.

transitive verb A verb that has an object.

U

uncountable noun A noun, such as 'milk', that is always singular because it can't be counted.

V

verb A word that describes an action or a state of being.

vowel One of the five letters: **a, e, i, o** and **u**.

W

word class The name for a type of word, such as a noun, a verb or an adjective.

Quiz answers

Page 13

1. **Spot the nouns:** 20 nouns: evening, Monday, September, break-in, bank, thieves, window, door, neighbour, noise, police, minutes, arrest, crime, alarm, money, injuries, men, car, police station.
2. **Proper or common?** Six proper nouns: Josh; Spain; Rufus; Wednesday; Peppers; Moira.
3. **Singular to plural:** watch > watches; foot > feet; deer > deer; tooth > teeth; potato > potatoes; kiss > kisses; person > people.

1. **Adding pronouns:** A strange creature was seen by Miss Kitty Keen as **she** walked to school with a friend. Later, **she** explained exactly what had happened. 'Finn and **I** had just entered the park when a creature stepped out in front of **us**. As **you** can imagine, **we** couldn't believe our eyes. Finn said **it** gave **him** a terrible shock.' Kitty went on to describe the creature. '**It** looked like a large cat, but **it** was covered in spots. **I** told Finn **I** was sure **it** was a leopard and **he** agreed with **me**. But when **we** told our parents **they** weren't convinced.'
2. **'I' or 'me'?:** Pronouns are used correctly in sentences 1 and 5.

Page 17

1. **Find the adjectives:** 12 adjectives: tired, frightened, hungry, steamy, thick, twisted, tangled, nasty, invisible, loud, deep, terrible.

Page 21

2. **Fill in the gaps:** 1. The **spooky** ghost story made us feel **scared**. 2. Hanif was so **tall** he could see over the **high** wall. 3. The cake was covered with **pink** icing and tasted very **sweet**.
3. **Making comparisons:** 2. The buffalo is heavy. The elephant is **heavier**. The whale is **the heaviest**. 3. The worm is slimy. The snail is **slimier**. The slug is **the slimiest**. 4. The dog is intelligent. The dolphin is **more intelligent**. The chimpanzee is **the most intelligent**.

Page 31

1. **Into the past:** Verbs in the past simple: swam; ran; found; played; felt; slept.
2. **Which tense? loves** = present simple; **has been playing** = present perfect continuous; **played** = past simple; **is playing** = present continuous; **will be joining** = future continuous; **will play** = future simple; **will have played** = future perfect.

1. **Active or passive?** Active sentences: 1, 3, 4. Passive sentences: 2, 5.
2. **Adding modal verbs:** 1. must; 2. ought; 3. should; 4. would; 5. have.

Page 35

1. **Spot the adverbs:** backwards, easily, very, yesterday, somewhere.
2. **Time, place, manner and degree:** Adverbs of time: early, never. Adverbs of place: here, indoors. Adverbs of manner: slowly, carefully. Adverbs of degree: rather, really.
3. **Fill in the gaps:** 1. straight; 2. hardly; 3. everywhere; 4. fast, late; 5. extremely; 6. passionately.

Page 39

Page 41

1. **Spot the prepositions:** Nine prepositions: over, through, in, across, round, past, up, to, on.
2. **Time, place or movement?** Prepositions of place: **at** the station; **in** the café; **on** the platform; **at** the view. Prepositions of time: **on** Monday night; **in** ten minutes; **past** midnight. Preposition of movement: racing **past** us.

Page 47

1. **Adding conjunctions:** We climbed the hill **because** we wanted to see the view, **but** the walk was very tiring. We kept on going **until** we got to the top. At last we reached a place **where** we could see the next valley. I took a quick look **and** climbed down the hill again.
2. **Which determiner?** 1. any; 2. the; 3. no; 4. my; 5. an; 6. many.

Page 53

1. **Simple, compound or complex?** Simple sentences: Eric loved fishing.; Then one day he felt a pull on his fishing line.
   Compound sentences: He went fishing every day, but he never caught anything.; He heaved with all his strength and he pulled out a boot!
   Complex sentences: Although he waited patiently for hours, nothing ever happened.; When Eric realized what he had caught, he was very disappointed.
2. **Main clause or subordinate clause?** Subordinate clauses: 1. who had trained for months; 2. because it was raining; 3. until Bernard came to stay; 4. If the rain stops; 5. that we were playing; 6. Although Kerry tried hard.

Quiz answers (continued)

Page 57

1. **Phrase or clause?** Phrases: across the desert; By the end of the day; every few minutes; Some of them; into the distance; In the end; under the stars. Clauses: until they could hardly move; as they walked; where they could sleep; wherever they looked.
2. **Adding phrases: My little sister** Molly has a **very unusual** pet. He is called Cedric and he lives **in a cardboard box. Last Monday**, Molly took Cedric **into the garden** and he escaped! He slithered **across the grass** and **under the fence**. Mrs Boggins, **our next-door neighbour,** spotted Cedric and screamed **in panic**. Molly had to promise that Cedric would not be allowed out **any more**.

1. **Direct to reported speech:** 1. I said it was too late. 2. Isabella said that she had done it earlier. 3. Mum told us to watch out. 4. Dad said that he would do it the next day. 5. Will asked if he could sit down.
2. **Making it direct:** 2. 'Sit down!' said Mrs Trott. 3. 'Don't eat any more cake,' said Dad. 4. 'My brother is ill,' said Fergus. 5. 'I can't come with you,' said Freya.

Page 63

1. **Making subjects and verbs agree:** 1. want; 2. Are; 3. were; 4. know; 5. was.
2. **Right or wrong?** The mistakes have been corrected in bold type: nobody **has** any idea about marking; someone always **drops** the ball. Everyone, including the supporters, **works** hard; the Barrington Battlers always **come** bottom of the league.

Page 67

1. **Fill in the gaps:** 1. me; 2. did; 3. sitting; 4. have; 5. its; 6. steak.
2. **Spot the mistakes:** The correct words are shown in bold type: **Whose** bicycle is this? **It's** covered with rust, the chain has come **loose,** and you need to change **those** tyres. If **you're** not careful you'll have an accident. **There** are lots of dangers out **there** and you might even run **into** a tree! Don't go out again until **it's passed its** safety test. I don't want to hear **any** excuses!

Page 75

Page 85

1. **Adding punctuation:** The correct punctuation marks have been added: The first time I met Oswin, we were on a hiking holiday. We had just climbed a long, steep and winding path. My legs ached, my feet hurt and my head throbbed painfully. Oswin, on the other hand, looked as fresh as a daisy.

   'What's the matter with you?' he asked.

   'I can't go on!' I replied.

2. **Commas needed:** Seven commas have been added: Jemima, my oldest friend, loves bags, watches and bangles. Her hair is thick, bright red and wavy. In the summer, she dances barefoot in the park. People often stare at her, but she doesn't care. In my opinion, she's the coolest girl in the school.

Page 93

1. **Making conversation:** 'I've got a surprise for you,' Kit said. 'Can you guess what it is?'

   'No. I can't,' I replied sleepily.

   'I'm sure you'll like it,' he said. 'Open your eyes,' he continued, 'and see what it is.' I opened my eyes and gasped.

   'I don't want a parrot!' I yelled.

2. **Adding apostrophes:** 1. He**'s** got his dad**'s** nose, has**n't** he? 2. Today**'s** the princess**'s** birthday. 3. The dog**'s** licking its paws. 4. Mo wo**n't** go to the children**'s** swimming classes.

3. **Find the right word:** 1. team's; 2. men's; 3. players'; 4. ships.

Page 101

1. **Adding brackets:** 1. I played tennis with Max (who is nearly fourteen) and I won! 2. On the way home, we spotted a snake. (I think it was an adder.) 3. We ate lychees (a kind of fruit) in China. 4. It took me ages to get home. (There was a rail strike.)

2. **Dashes needed:** Ellie has moved to France – I don't know why. She packed up all her stuff – books, posters and clothes – before she left. She didn't tell us she was going – it was a big surprise. We waited for a month – which seemed more like a year – before we heard any news. Then suddenly, it arrived – a postcard from Paris!

3. **Missing hyphens:** My **laid-back** brother loves **do-it-yourself** projects. Our house is full of his badly made, **broken-down** furniture. Mum says he should smarten up. She's tired of his **couldn't-care-less** attitude.

Index

Index (continued)

R

relative clauses
see **clauses**
reported speech 58-62,
  80, 129
rhetorical questions 81

S

sat/stood 69
semicolon 89, 129
sentences 48-51, 110-111,
  120-121
  complex sentences
    51, 126
  compound sentences
    51, 126
  sentence fragments 49
  simple sentences 51,
    129
shall 29
shortened words 72-73,
  78, 81, 90, 115
should 32, 68
simile 109, 129
slang 104-105
social media 100
some 66
spelling 10, 12, 19, 37,
  116-119, 124
subject 15, 22-23, 34,
  56, 64-66, 120-121, 129
subject-verb agreement
  64-66
subordinate clauses
  see **clauses**

suffixes 118-119, 129
superlatives 19-20, 129
syllables 20, 119, 129
synonyms 106-107, 129

T

take/bring 69
teach/learn 68
tenses *see* **verb tenses**
them 70
they're/their/there 72
time 114
transitive verbs *see* **verbs**

U

uncountable nouns
  see **nouns**

V

verbal noun 124
verbs 6-7, 22-30, 32-34,
  64-66, 97, 120-124, 129
  auxiliary verbs 27, 32,
    123, 125
  inflection 122, 127
  intransitive verbs 23, 33,
    122, 127
  irregular verbs 24, 26,
    123
  modal verbs 32, 127
  phrasal verbs 33, 97,
    122, 128
  transitive verbs 23, 33,
    122, 129

verb tenses 24-30, 59-60,
  129
  future continuous 28, 30
  future perfect 28, 30
  future perfect
    continuous 29, 30
  future simple 28, 30
  past continuous 25,
    30, 59
  past perfect 26, 30, 59
  past perfect continuous
    27, 30
  past simple 24, 30, 59,
    122, 123
  present continuous 25,
    30, 59
  present perfect 26,
    30, 59
  present perfect
    continuous 27, 30
  present simple 24,
    30, 59
vowels 45, 116, 119, 129

W

whether/if 61
who/whom 52
who's/whose 73
will 28-30, 32, 60
word classes 6-7, 47, 129
would 60, 68

Y

you're/your 73